Welcome...

In the 1980s the car you drove said more about you than almost anything else could. And it had become easier to get the cars you wanted, courtesy of the advent of easy finance and the growing acceptance of the idea that a car was a fashion item rather than a lifetime investment. With designs growing more daring and the needs of the average family shifting, it was a more interesting time for car buyers than ever before. And while some 1970s relics were still on sale, most manufacturers embraced the new era with new designs and drivetrains.

What you drove – or what your parents had – mattered, and the manufacturers knew it. And this makes the 1980s one of the most important decades in motoring, and one responsible for more motoring memories than almost any other. Whether you were a back seat passenger in Dad's Senator or you took to the roads for the first time in your very own Peugeot 205, the motoring memories of a decade have arguably shaped the way we see the roads ever since.

And that's what this bookazine is all about – family cars to suit all tastes and budgets from a decade that was pivotal in terms of

automotive culture. This is a nostalgic look back at the cars that we, our parents, and our grandparents drove while raising their families. We hope you enjoy reading it as much as we enjoyed producing it.

Sam Skelton
Editor

CONTENTS...

ISBN: 978 1 83632 188 0
Editor: Sam Skelton
Image credits: Sam Skelton
Richard Gunn
Wikimedia Commons (under Creative Commons licence
www.creativecommons.org/licenses/by/2.0/deed.en)
Senior editor, specials:
Roger Mortimer
Email: roger.mortimer@keypublishing.com
Production and design: Panda Media
Advertising Sales Manager: Sam Clark
Email: sam.clark@keypublishing.com
Tel: 01780 755131

Advertising production:
Becky Antoniades
Email: rebecca.antoniades@keypublishing.com

SUBSCRIPTION/MAIL ORDER
Key Publishing Ltd, PO Box 300, Stamford, Lincs, PE9 1NA
Tel: 01780 480404
Subscriptions email:
subs@keypublishing.com
Mail Order email: orders@keypublishing.com
Website: www.keypublishing.com/shop

PUBLISHING
Group CEO: Adrian Cox
Publisher: Steve O'Hara

Published by
Key Publishing Ltd,
PO Box 100, Stamford, Lincs, PE9 1XQ
Tel: 01780 755131
Website: www.keypublishing.com

PRINTING
Precision Colour Printing Ltd, Haldane,
Halesfield 1, Telford, Shropshire. TF7 4QQ

DISTRIBUTION
Seymour Distribution Ltd,
2 Poultry Avenue, London, EC1A 9PU
Enquiries Line: 02074 294000.

Peugeot 205

The supermini that showed all the others it was possible to be sensible AND cool.

There was only really one car that could claim to hold the title of the best hot hatch in the world – and shockingly, it wasn't the Volkswagen Golf. The pretender, smaller and yet with bigger and more powerful engines by the end of its life, offered the same sort of nippy handling that rose tinted apologists ascribe to the Mini along with rocketship performance. So what if it felt a bit flimsy – that just made it feel more dangerous, and thus much more fun. The Peugeot 205 GTi was an icon of the era. And everybody wanted to own one.

Even if the closest you got was the 1.1 your driving instructor had, or the 1.4GR your mum had, or even the little diesel van variant you might have driven for work. Because they all had one thing in common – a truly excellent little chassis that would take everything you threw at it and come back asking for more.

Because the Peugeot 205 was that rare thing, it could be all things to all men. From diesels that could teach a Yorkshireman the value of parsimony to leather and walnut lined Gentry models with metallic paint, an automatic gearbox and alloy wheels, there was a 205 you could make fit well into any sort of lifestyle. Pert and pretty courtesy of Pininfarina it was popular with all ages. There was even a cute little convertible available in CJ and CTi variants, for fans of the diminutive Pug who wanted the wind in their hairspray.

It was all so much better than the cars which came before – and there were plenty of those to choose from. Because the Peugeot 104 was never a strong seller in Britain despite a perfectly worthy image, and the 104ZS Coupe frankly looked odd owing to its chopped down wheelbase. Sister company Citroën might have offered the five door Visa, but with styling only its mother could love and a traditionally soft Gallic ride it wasn't the supermini to vanquish rivals from Ford and Vauxhall. As for the halfway-house Talbot Samba, it might have been the closest thing to a success for the 104 chassis in Britain but it had all the street cred of corduroy. There might have been a convertible version of that too, but its association with dead end driveway

Even if you couldn't afford a GTi, every 205 offered style and good handling.

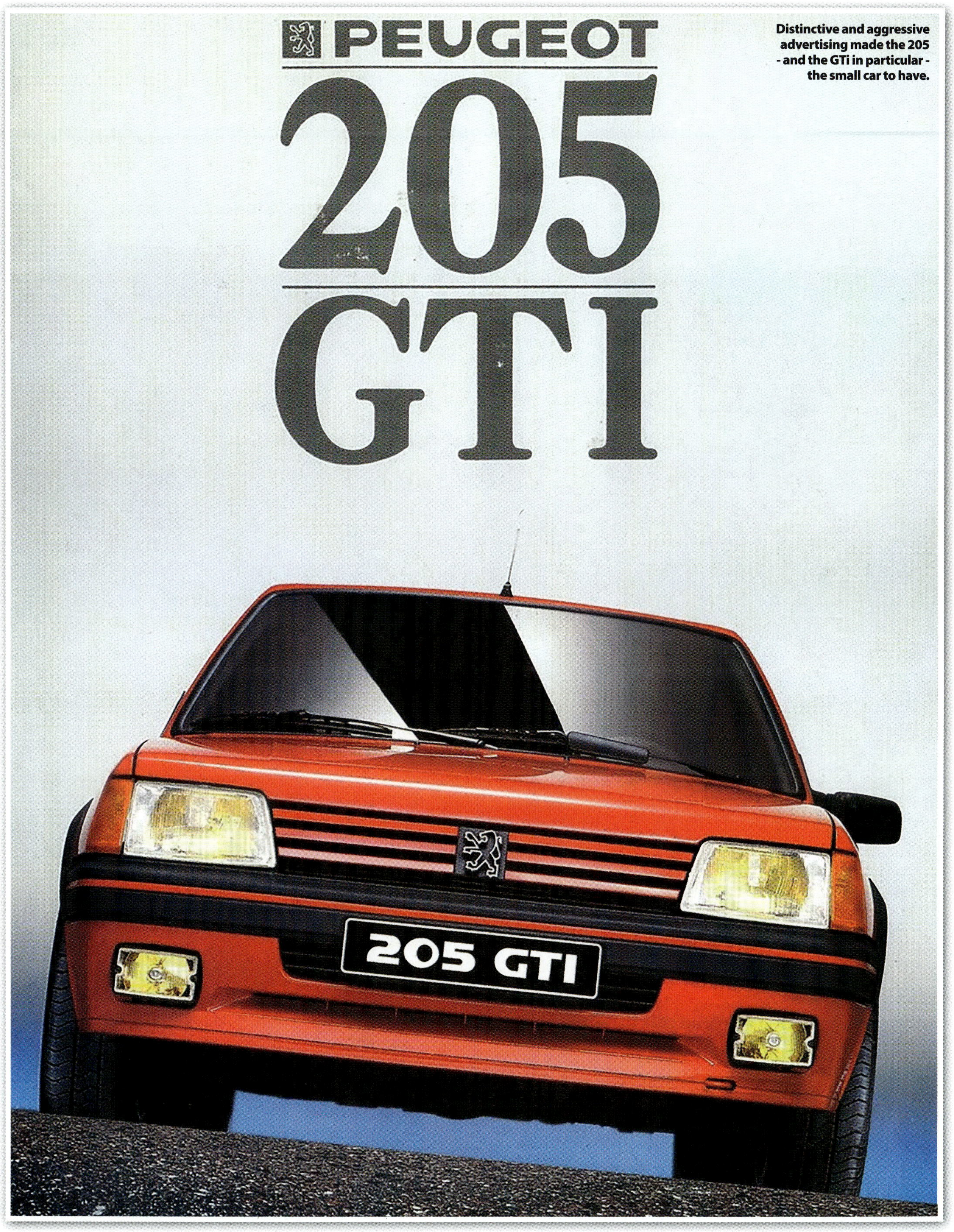

Distinctive and aggressive advertising made the 205 - and the GTi in particular - the small car to have.

dustbins like the Alpine and Tagora meant that the one thing the Samba could never hope to be – not with all the Rallye badges and rorty 1.4 engines in the world – was cool.

The 205 wasn't expensive either. A 954cc 205XE could be yours for £4145 in 1985, barely more than a Mini and a much more modern proposition, even if it had a tiny engine. The 1.4XT at £5895 and the 1.4GT at £6345 were the priciest options in the mainstream range, comparable with top end Metros or the equally pert Renault 5. The GTi 1.6 at £7145 was a grand cheaper than the Golf GTi and almost £500 cheaper than the Escort XR3i, but had the power to match both in a more compact and light package. It might have been more expensive than the

similarly sized MG Metro Turbo but it was so much more car.

A combination of its style, price and availability meant that the 205 swiftly became the car of choice for all self-respecting petrolheads upon passing their driving tests. A Junior or a GE might not have had the same sort of power as the GTi, but that didn't stop it being just as entertaining in the right hands on the right road. You might not have had 115bhp under your right foot – or even 130bhp, if the GTi you admired most was the later 1.9 – but show even the sub 1.0 models a twisting B road and take some brave pills and you could have very nearly as much fun hurling it into the bends at speed and learning all about lift off oversteer the hard way. And if you wanted the look, just head to the nearest scrapyard, find a GTi that some overexuberant idiot had parked around a tree, and swap the bits

Five door models have been mostly forgotten today, but lent the 205 even greater practicality than the three door original.

The CTi - an open GTi - effectively rendered the sports car obsolete.

The CJ may not have had the CTi's engine, but its 1.4-litre unit didn't detract from its charm.

The GT was a warm and well specced variant - its three door equivalent was the XS.

across for a Junior GTi without the power.

They were endearingly French in other ways too – the trim quality was crap but the basics were well put together – so you might lose some of your plastics but the cars would fundamentally last forever. 205s didn't even rust as badly as the average small cars, adding to their potential for longevity. It was hard to find a cheaper mode of transport than a secondhand 205 when you factored in its likely lifespan, especially if you managed to get hold of one of the cars fitted with the 1.8-litre XUD diesel engine. It might have been a heavy lump for the car and increased its propensity to understeer but by doing comfortably north of 45mpg regardless of how it was driven it endeared itself to people who saw basic spending as profligacy and valued parsimony over all attributes. To this day in rural France you will still see battered 205 diesels doing the job that was always meant for them. ■

	Peugeot 205 1.1GL	Peugeot 205 1.4GR	Peugeot 205GTi 1.6	Peugeot 205GTi 1.9	Peugeot 205 D Turbo
CAPACITY	1124cc	1360cc	1580cc	1905cc	1769cc
POWER	55bhp	59bhp	115bhp	130bhp	78bhp
TORQUE	64lb.ft	78lb.ft	98lb.ft	119lb.ft	84lb.ft
TOP SPEED	99mph	100mph	122mph	123mph	103mph

austin metro

Let's be honest, the Mini was out of date by 1980. The Metro was meant to carry its torch forward.

A British Car To Beat The World. So read the advertising copy when the Metro was unveiled in 1980. And while it didn't quite drive all those pesky little foreign superminis back into the sea in the way the television ads suggested, it was a definite hit with British buyers, never dropping below 6th in the top ten new car sales charts until the Austin variant was replaced in 1990 by a shiny new model with Rover badging. And while the dear old Metro had its faults, all those driving instructors and blue rinsers couldn't be wrong.

In an industry where the average model has a lifespan of eight to ten years, for the Mini to have made it to 21 years old by 1980 was an incredible feat. And it's entirely understandable that the market was moving on – it may still have been Britain's fourth best selling car but it had been overtaken in small car terms by the Ford Fiesta, and the Vauxhall Chevette was giving it something to worry about too. BL had been trying to replace the Mini for most of the 1970s, starting with the Clubman program and

Vanden Plas models showed that you could have a small car with luxury features, just like the 1960s Mini-based Wolseley Hornet.

trying more daring projects such as the 9X behind closed doors. The project developed greater traction during the 1970s, and the resultant Austin miniMetro of 1980 – as those first models

were called – was launched to critical acclaim from the press. The miniMetro name was soon dropped in favour of Metro – BL having been forbidden from using the Metro name on its own by rail

manufacturer Metro-Cammell. As the popularity of the car took off, both parties forgot about the agreement and the Metro wore the name it had always been meant to wear.

Austin Morris

Justifiably billed as 'a British car to beat the world', the new Metro offers all-purpose versatility, from its exceptionally roomy interior, lively performance, quiet, refined ride, extremely low running costs and consistently high quality. Built by microprocessor-controlled robots in Europe's most advanced assembly plant, the Metro is the ideal family car of the 80's.

Running costs are reduced by the car's aerodynamically efficient styling, by its low fuel consumption, by 12,000 mile—or once a year—servicing intervals, by its low insurance rating from such money-saving features as bolt-on front wings.

There are five models in the Metro range. All but one (the standard Metro) feature a unique Split Action rear seat, comprising a single and a double

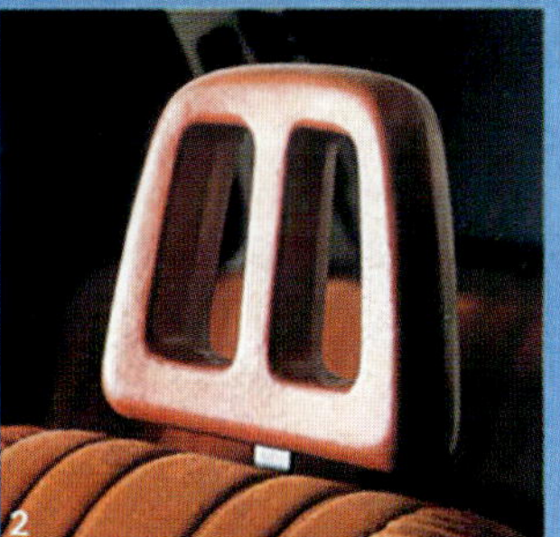

1. Top three Metros— 1.3S, HLE, 1.3HLS

2. Distinctive HLS head restraints

3. Neat, compact HLS fascia

4. Stylish HLS interior

Engine:
Four-cylinder, transverse, o.h.v. 'A Plus' engine in unit with clutch, gearbox and final drive. *(Standard, L and HLE models):* Capacity 998 cc (60.96 in³), *44 b.h.p. at 5,250 rev/min on Standard and L models: *47 b.h.p. at 5,500 rev/min on HLE model. *(1,3 S and 1,3 HLS models):* Capacity 1,275 cc (77,8 in³), *63 b.h.p. at 5,600 rev/min.

Transmission:
Diaphragm spring clutch. Four forward speed synchromesh gearbox. Front wheel drive, open shafts.

Steering:
Rack and pinion.

Road Wheels:
Five pressed steel with steel braced radial tyres; size: 135SR—12 on Standard, L and HLE models, 155/70SR—12 on 1.3 S and 1.3 HLS models.

Suspension:
Independent †Hydragas system.

* DIN 70020
† Registered Trademark

Brochures focused on the model's wholesome good sense.

Not quite as space-conscious as the Mini had been, but well-packaged nonetheless.

And British Leyland was quick to capitalise on the model in the same way that it had with the Mini two decades earlier – and using the same tactics. The sporting Cooper idea – despite Cooper having developed a hot Metro – was taken in house, badged an MG, and showered with more red goodies than a Labour party conference. From 1982, the newly-named Austin Rover even cottoned on to the latest 1980s power craze and bolted a turbocharger on to the MG Metro to produce the fastest pocket rocket of its era. The Riley Elf and Wolseley Hornet had sold well enough, so BL took the Metro, stuffed it full of wood and soft tweed, chucked some chrome on it and called it a Vanden Plas, marketing it as the model for people "with an interior motive" and later throwing leather trim into the mix to boot with the limited edition Vanden Plas 500 model.

So what if its Hydragas suspension had been compromised by Spen King's "Not Invented Here" policies, effectively isolating the damper units at the front and linking sideways at the back to rob the car of the ride it could have had? (Hydragas's inventor, Dr Alex Moulton, created a Metro with the suspension properly interlinked. After King was forced to drive it one day, the subsequent Rover Metro's underpinnings would be put right.) And so what if its seats

Metro vans were originally sold as Morrises, but by the Mk2 pictured here had reverted to the Austin brand.

Metro Turbo was a real pocket rocket.

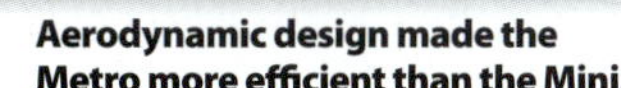

Aerodynamic design made the Metro more efficient than the Mini.

Special editions helped to keep the Metro fresh.

guaranteed jobs for osteopaths and its low quality steel kept welders in work? In those early months, none of it really mattered. For the first time in over a decade British Leyland had a car that could realistically take on its rivals, a car that wasn't hopelessly dated – and with patronage from Lady Diana Spencer, it had the right image too.

That is, until the pension book posse started buying them. Because you could doll the Metro up with all the red carpets, MG badges and turbochargers you liked, you could fit a leather and walnut interior, but ultimately nobody chose to be seen in a car beloved by the bowls club. The Metro was a perfectly worthy little thing, but the Fiesta and the Nova had much more street cred. There is however a lot of power in the grey pound, and the Metro's sales figures made it a definite success for British Leyland despite its image problems. In 1981 the Metro was Britain's fourth best-selling car, just behind the Ford Fiesta. In 1982 and 1983 it overtook the Fiesta for the third place spot. By 1984 it had dropped to fourth, fifth by 1986, fourth again for 1987 and sixth for 1989. For its entire production life It sat within the top ten, and was either Britain's first or second best selling supermini.

In 1984, BL tried to improve matters with a facelift and then a new five door option, beating competition such as the Ford Fiesta and the Volkswagen Polo to the easy access game. While the Metro didn't survive the purge of the Austin brand unscathed – with a lazy facelift and a new shield shaped grille badge – the market knew that a new and better Metro was coming. The K-series engined models of 1989 might have looked similar to what had come before, but there were enough changes inside and out for Rover finally to admit the model to its main range and bring it in from the cold, leaving only the Maestro and Montego as brand orphans following the end of Austin badging. ∎

	Austin Metro 1.0	Austin Metro 1.3	MG Metro 1300	MG Metro Turbo
CAPACITY	998cc	1275cc	1275cc	1275cc
POWER	41bhp	62bhp	72bhp	93bhp
TORQUE	51lb.ft	72lb.ft	73lb.ft	85lb.ft
TOP SPEED	87mph	95mph	103mph	111mph

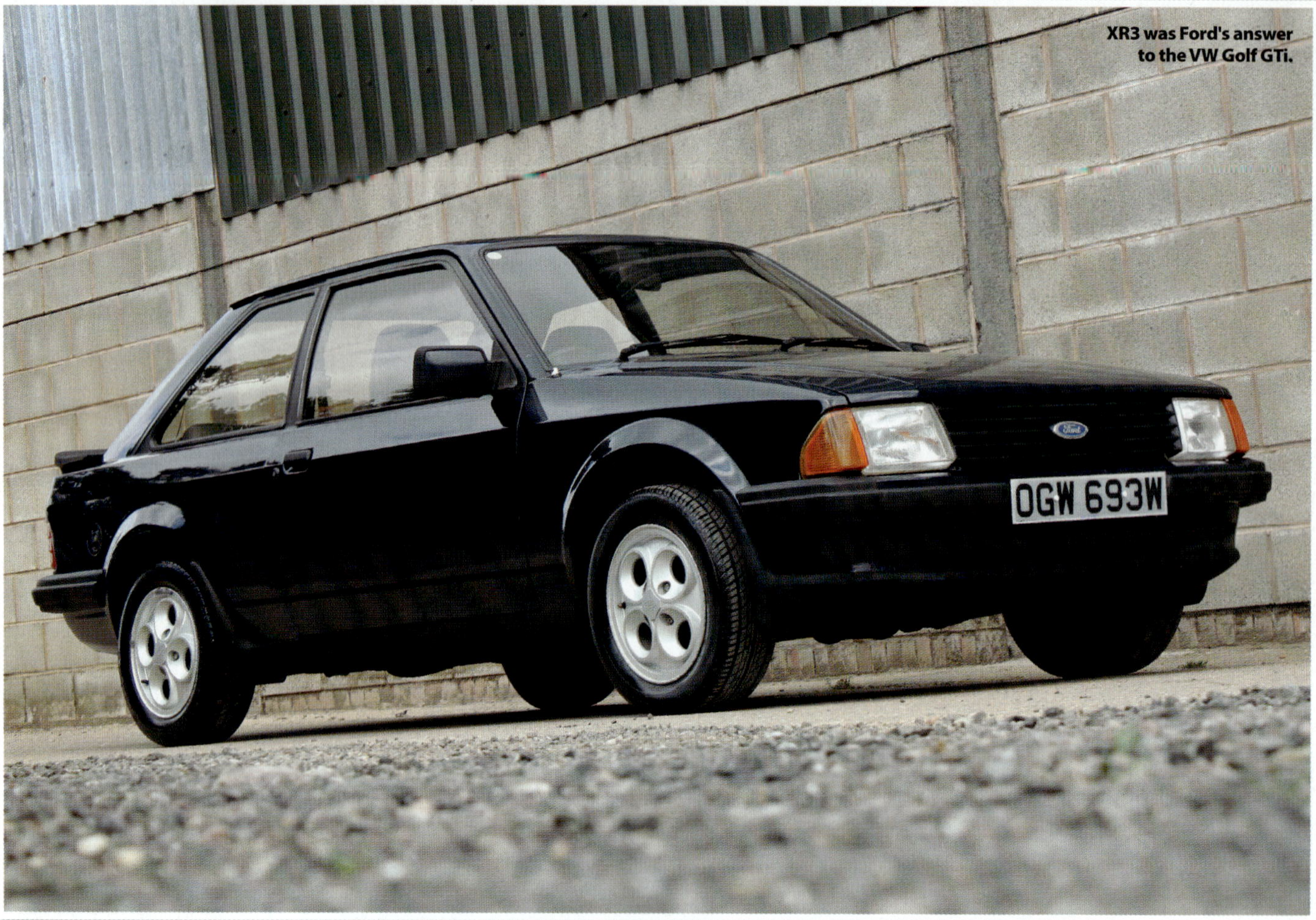

XR3 was Ford's answer to the VW Golf GTi.

Ford Escort Mk3

Ford's family friendly front driver might have been controversial, but it met the market needs perfectly.

It's fair to say that the Volkswagen Golf caught the rest of the small family car manufacturers napping. The small and upmarket front wheel drive hatchback was something new – particularly in Britain where the traditional idea of a hatchback was the dreadfully well-meaning Austin Maxi. It was about as desirable on the showroom floor as the well-meaning local vicar at a rock concert, and the average family car buyer stuck firmly to rear wheel drive saloons until something better came along. In the Golf, the buying public had that, and with the tide starting to turn Ford knew that its next Escort would have to be a car in the Golf mould. Not only that, but its swish new supermini the Fiesta had been hoovering up sales in the Mini and Polo class, making an Escort which copied the smaller car's basic formula a clever move. As a result the Mk3

Standard Escorts were less dramatic in appearance, but just as practical.

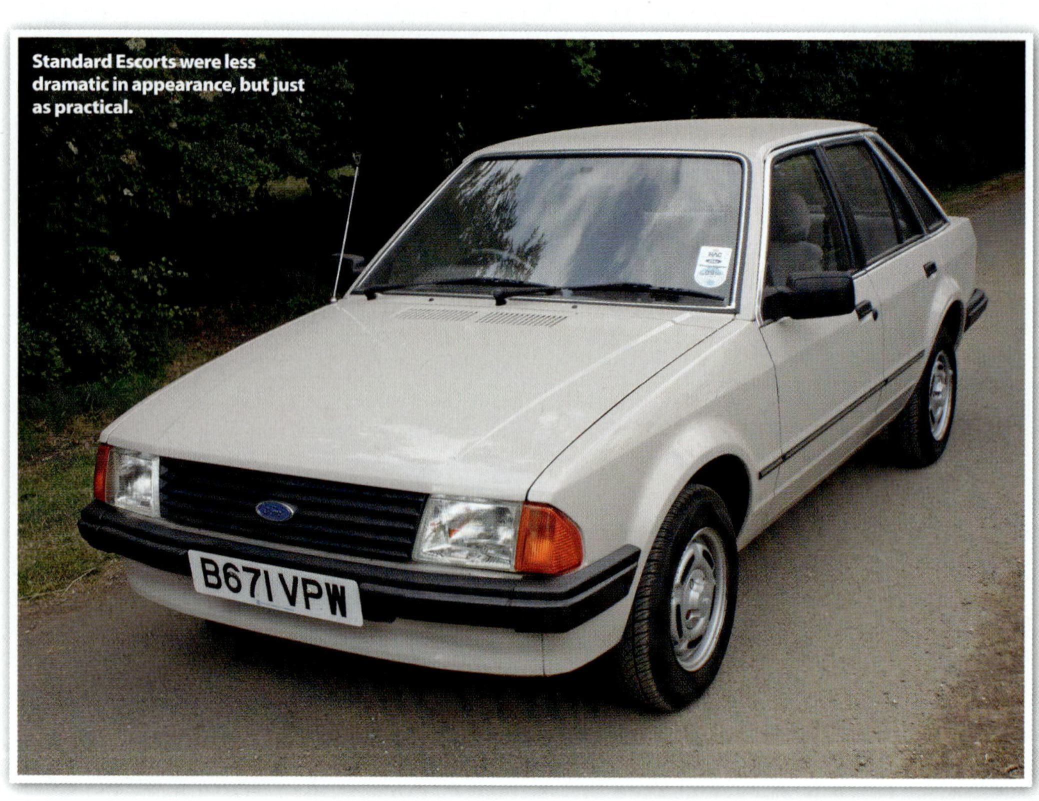

Early Cabriolets were available in 1.6 (pictured) and 1.6i guise.

Orion was intended to recapture sales lost by the larger Sierra.

Escort of 1980 would be front wheel drive. It would also be a hatchback – though with a hint of a bustle-back to reassure buyers not yet ready to transition from a saloon. "Simple is efficient" read the advertising copy – and Ford went out of its way to ensure that the buying public knew that this new two box shape with its front wheel drive layout was as simple as it could get.

Through a combination of the Golf's success and Ford's dealer network, the public saw the new Escort mostly as it was – though there was a small subsection of the former Escort market that viewed the hatchback concept with deep suspicion. While in the early days of the new model Ford would simply upsell this clientele into a Cortina, but after the disastrous launch of the Sierra that was no longer an option. For these people – and for those who found the Sierra just a little too far out – Ford developed a four door saloon variant of the Escort in the same sort of vein as Volkswagen's Golf-based Jetta. This new car, the Orion, was only available in upmarket trim levels at launch, reflecting its position as a premium alternative.

And the tactic worked. With the Escort, Ford managed to retain a much higher market share than it had with the more mechanically conservative Sierra simply by managing the launch and ensuring options remained available for those who weren't yet willing to take a step into the unknown. By making the Escort look more familiar and retaining the option for a four door saloon, it mitigated any risk that came from tampering with the Escort formula – and while the Mk3 Escort wasn't exactly inspiring, it did shift people's perception of what a family Ford ought to be. From basic Bonus models to the relatively opulent Ghia, three and five door hatchbacks and estates, there was an Escort to suit all pockets and requirements, though the mid range 1.3L and 1.6GL were the most popular sellers of the range. In trade? You'd want one of the two Escort vans –based on the estate and in box van form, to rival the Bedford Astravan and Astramax.

There was even a hot Escort with a hot new name. Gone were the days of cars like the RS2000 where Ford simply stuck the biggest Cortina engine into the Escort – because the 2.0 Pinto wasn't suitable for the new front wheel drive layout. Instead, the new CVH engine fitted to the top of the line 1600s were fitted with a nice twin choke Weber, the car sprouted some extra black trim, and the steel wheels gave way to an unusual cloverleaf design of alloy. The

	Ford Escort 1.3	Ford Orion 1.4	Ford Escort 1.6	Ford Escort XR3	Ford Orion 1600E	Ford Escort 1.6i Cabrio
CAPACITY	1296cc	1392cc	1597cc	1597cc	1597cc	1597cc
POWER	70bhp	75bhp	79bhp	96bhp	105bhp	105bhp
TORQUE	74lb.ft	80lb.ft	92lb.ft	98lb.ft	101lb.ft	101lb.ft
TOP SPEED	98mph	104mph	103mph	113mph	118mph	116mph

Mk4 facelift brought Sierra style swoopiness.

XR3 not only had the Golf GTi in its sights, but it sold for more money than the Volkswagen. Further performance models would follow in typical Ford style – the fuel injected XR3i, the limited run RS1600i and the later, turbocharged RS Turbo model.

Ford also gave us a convertible variant – sold initially as the 1.6 to Ghia specification and the 1.6i to XR3i spec, but sold as the XR3i cabriolet from 1986 onwards. That same year the Escort underwent a mid term facelift – unofficially attracting a new "mark" designation. The Mk4 – as it was known to the public – had a new mostly-enclosed grille and smoother detailing in a bid to emulate the Sierra – by now mostly accepted, as its novelty value had eroded and fleet buyers had recognised that underneath sat fundamentally the same simple package.

Estate models offered space aplenty.

But where Ford had got it mostly right with the Mk3, it failed to do so when it launched the car's replacement in 1990. The new Mk5 Escort had a more aerodynamic, Sierra-esque shell, but unfortunately, this was the only aspect of the design that was really updated – the rear suspension was a retrograde step, with a torsion beam in place of the independent setup from the Mk3, the engines were the same coarse CVHs as the old model, and it rode and handled as if Ford hadn't tried. Held up by motoring historians as a prime example of why car designers shouldn't simply listen to what a focus group says it wants, the Mk5 Escort underwent a thorough mechanical revision and facelift just two years into production in order to make it into the car Ford should have put on sale in the first place. ∎

The facelift particularly suited Cabriolet models.

vauxhall astra

More interesting than an Escort, the Vauxhall Astra range had something for everyone.

Students of Vauxhall and Opel in the 1960s and 1970s could be forgiven for a little confusion. The Opel Kadett A and Vauxhall Viva HA had been sisters under the skin, though the models had subsequently diverged to cater for their respective markets. Kadett B and Vivas HB and HC were therefore separate models, but General Motors' plan for a world small car meant that Vauxhall would be launching a variant of the car Opel would turn into the Kadett C; the Chevette. Obvious then that it would replace the Viva, yes? No – instead it became an entry level model, sitting below the car it might otherwise have replaced. The Viva would be replaced with a car based on the Kadett C's replacement, the Kadett D. And yet, this Astra would not replace the Chevette, which continued alongside the newer car in its entry position.

Confusing, we can all agree. But in the wake of Volkswagen's Golf, Vauxhall was keen that its new model wasn't seen as a mere entry level proposition. By retaining the Chevette in its range as an entry level product Vauxhall was able to pitch the Astra as a premium model to steal sales from the Golf. After all, it had an equally German heritage – but a badge that Anglophiles would want on the driveway. British Astras came in two flavours at first – 1.3S GL five door hatchback and 1.3S L five door estate, pitched cleverly at £4,602 and £4,373 respectively. Not only was this higher than the Chevette, but almost as high as the Cavalier 1.6GL four door. Pitching the Astra as more expensive than the Golf GLS made a brave statement, but led rivals Ford into a trap; when it launched its own new small family hatchback to target the Golf and Astra it pitched it at an even higher price point. At the same time, Vauxhal expanded its range downward – making the car people perceived as a Golf competitor into the best value option of the three. Not that the cheaper Astras offered the same flexibility; despite looking identical on the surface the entry level models were two and four door saloons. But by then it had the premium image, and buyers were happy to be able to afford it at all even if that meant sacrificing some practicality in the process.

Vauxhall really got into its stride with the aerodynamically-focused Mk2 Astra of 1984,

At launch, just two models were available.

though – with its teardrop shape hiding more space. Like the Chevette of the 1970s, the Kadett E and Astra Mk2 were part of a GM World Car project, with developments built in Korea as the Daewoo Le Mans, exported to America as the Pontiac Le Mans, and sold in Canada under the Asuna and Passport brands. Launched as a pair of three and five door hatchbacks, a corresponding pair of three and five door estates and a Bedford branded van based on the three door estate, the range would grow with saloon, convertible and box van variants. Two of these new Astra derivatives would reach the pinnacle of automotive culture in the UK, legends in their time and not necessarily in a positive way. First there was the Vauxhall Belmont – a four door Astra targeted squarely at Jetta and Orion buyers, with a cavernous boot and improved specifications. Popular with elderly motorists and often left unsecured, the Belmont would spend the early part of

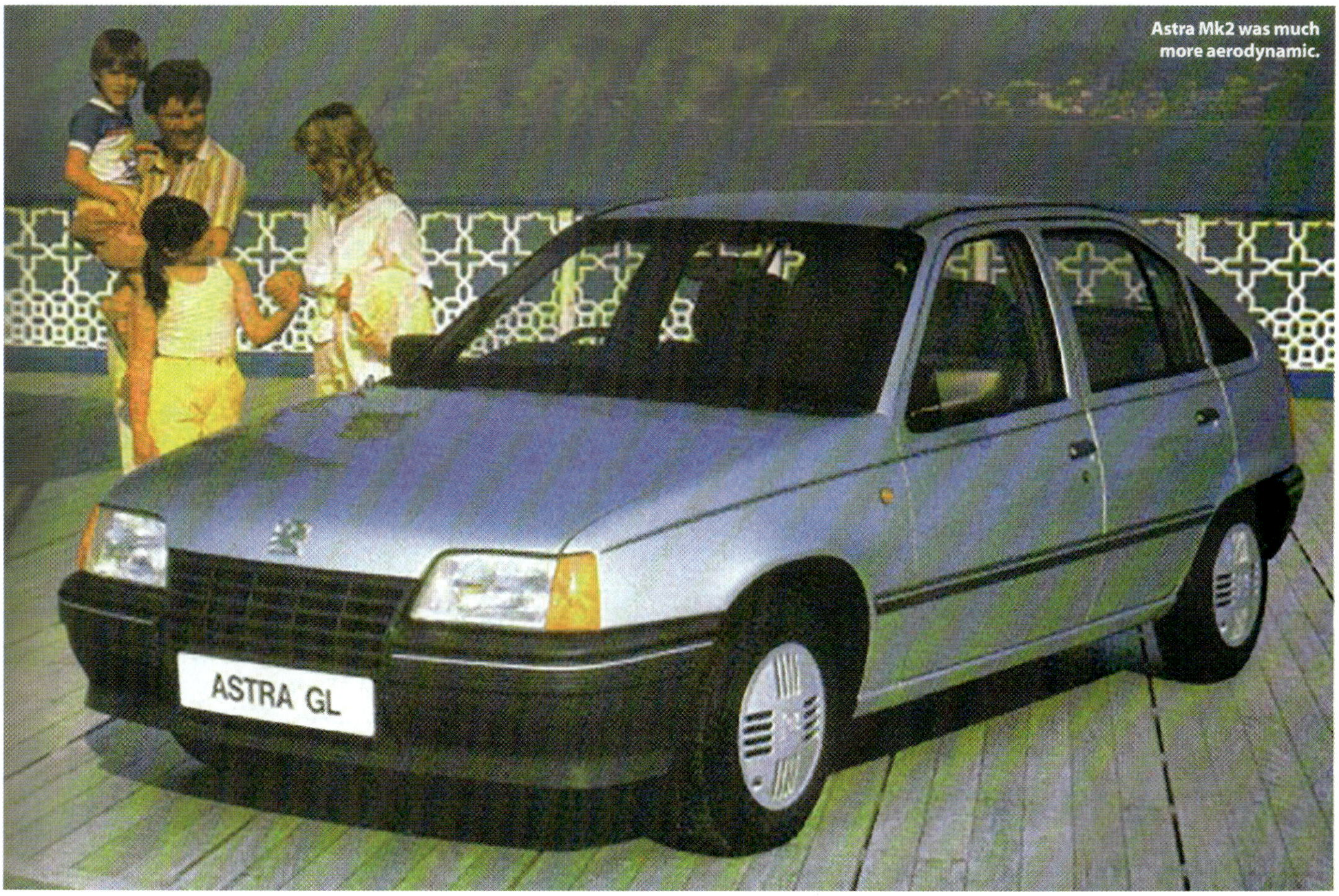

Astra Mk2 was much more aerodynamic.

ASTRA GL

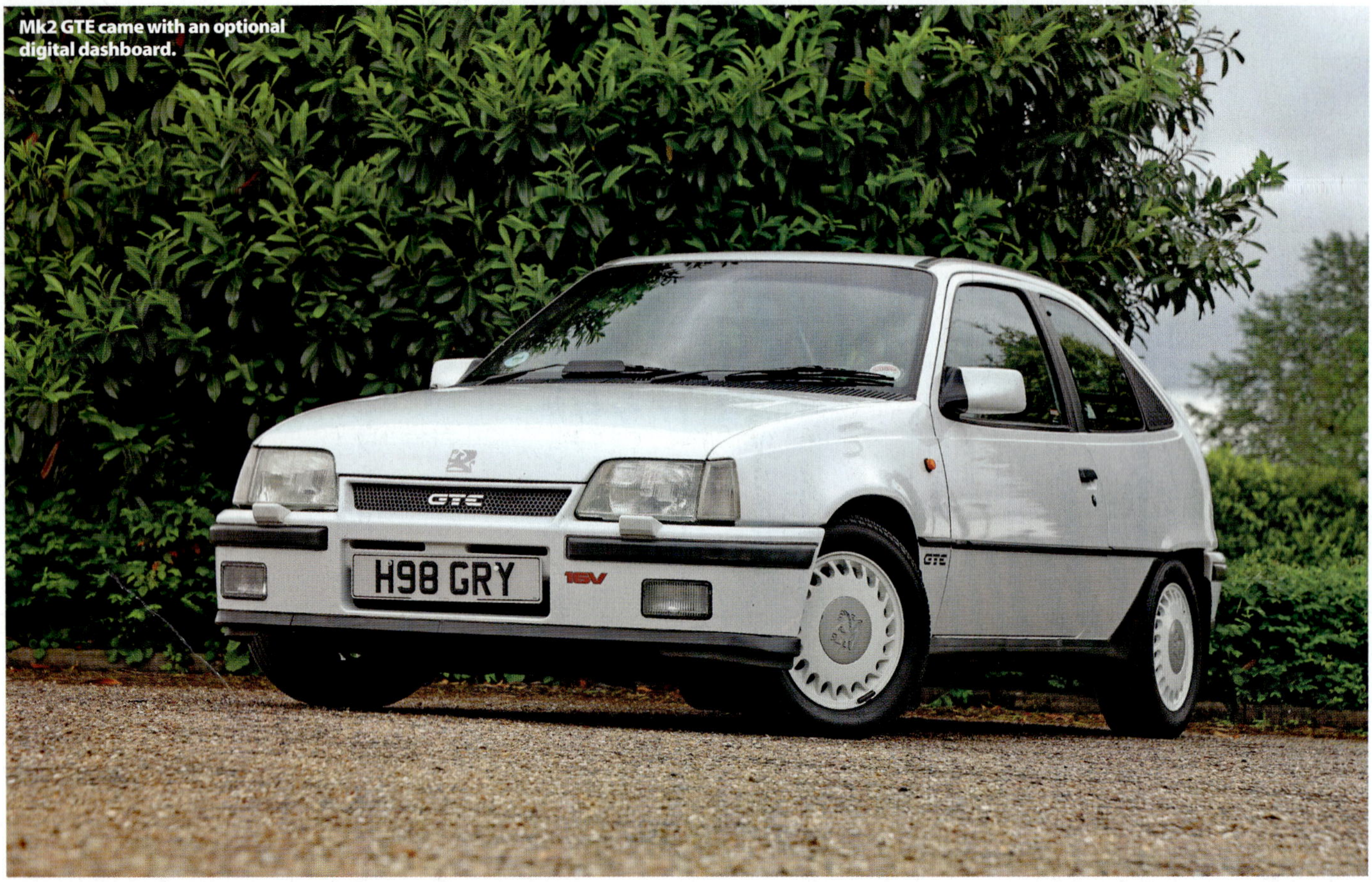

Mk2 GTE came with an optional digital dashboard.

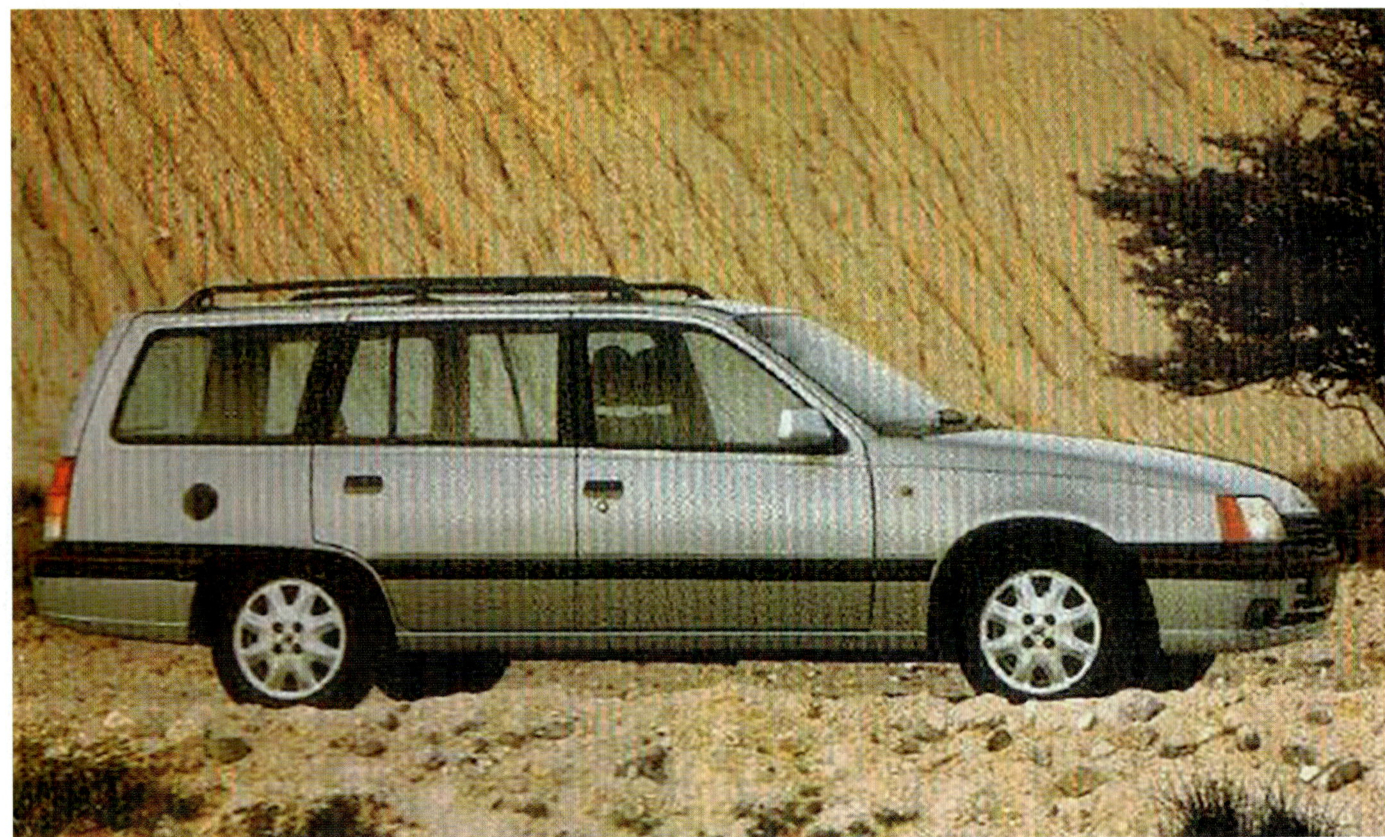

the 2000s with the undesirable sobriquet of Britain's most stolen vehicle, with 1978 Belmonts stolen in Britain in 2003 – one in ten Belmonts had been stolen during that timeframe. And the second – albeit unofficial – title earned by a Mk2 Astra derivative was earned by the larger of its two van models, the Bedford Astramax. Because between its introduction in 1985 and the end of the century it was hard to look in your mirror in Britain without seeing a demented plumber in an Astramax desperate to get past. This combined with the way they were driven on dual carriageways led to the unofficial crown as Britain's fastest road vehicle – because whatever you were driving from Reliant to Ferrari, you could never escape the Astramax in the mirror…

Not content with soaking itself into popular culture, the Astra Mk2 insinuated itself onto the driveways of millions of families up and down the country, climbing the UK best-sellers list from number 7 to number 5 and selling in

Belmont LXi was the only Belmont estate, and one of Vauxhall's rarest models.

Astra convertible was a popular alternative to the Escort Cabriolet.

Once Britain's most stolen car, the Belmont saloon was ideal for those needing a bigger boot than the Astra.

excess of 100,000 per annum on average from 1985 to 1990. There were commodious estates, upmarket big engined Belmont CDs, humble little three door Merits and even a convertible for the family who liked open air thrills. Oddities in the range included the Belmont LXi estate of 1989 - the only estate not to be badged as an Astra, its blacked out pillars and mini Carlton grille showed that it was intended as a more luxurious model. The LXi was fundamentally an SRi estate by another name, targeted to avoid sullying the sporting brand by associating it with a carryall – few were sold, fewer survive, and few really care. The model would be binned off when, in the last 12 months of Mk2 Astra production, all SRi and LXi models were renamed SXi. By 1991 there would be a newer, sleeker Astra replacing all variants barring the convertible, though the older model would return to the market for 1995 bearing Daewoo Nexia branding. ■

	Vauxhall Astra Mk1 1.6	Vauxhall Astra Mk1 GTE	Vauxhall Astra Mk2 1.3	Vauxhall Astra Mk2 1.6	Vauxhall Belmont GLSi
CAPACITY	1598cc	1796cc	1297cc	1598cc	1796cc
POWER	90bhp	113bhp	75bhp	90bhp	115bhp
TORQUE	93lb.ft	111lb.ft	75lb.ft	93lb.ft	111lb.ft
TOP SPEED	108mph	118mph	105mph	105mph	120mph

VW wisely chose not to mess too much with the Golf formula.

vw golf and jetta

Simple, trustworthy and well built, the Golf and its Jetta sibling were the targets to which all other manufacturers aspired.

You have to wonder what was going on in Volkswagen's ad department in the 1980s. If we were to believe the television, a Golf driver was the sort of person who might put a million on black, only for it to come up red. Who married a sex kitten right as she became a cat. (Aside – was this the woman from the other 80s Golf ad?) Who invested in commodities right as everyone else moved out. While the thrust of the advert was that everyone needed something to rely on and for this man it was his Volkswagen, frankly the message it sent was that you'd have to be an utter moron to want to drive one. This wasn't Doyle Dane Bernbach self deprecation like the Beetle ads of the 50s, this was out and out idiocy.

Especially as there was nothing idiotic about the car being advertised. The first Golf of 1974 had been the car the company needed to replace the Beetle – it was up to the minute, compact, practical, and that Giugiaro-designed body looked good when put alongside cars like the Austin Allegro and the Ford Escort. It also begat the Golf GTi, the car that arguably invented the modern concept of the hot hatchback, Claimed by many in the motoring press to be the most complete car of all time, it melded fashionable styling with sensible economy and sportscar-beating speed. It was desirable, flash, yet good value, and it appealed to everyone from young farmers to the Sloane Street in-crowd. But having spent the 1970s with the market to itself, other manufacturers had

caught on to the possibilities that a small family hatchback could offer, and both Ford and Vauxhall had replaced their small saloons with hatchbacks by the time the Golf was due to be replaced. When it came to succeeding the Mk1, Volkswagen knew that there was only one sensible thing to do – and as the Golf was a sensible car, the sensible option made most sense.

So the next Golf was fundamentally a clone of what had come before. A little longer, a little wider, a little more refined and comfortable. And the same principles applied to the new version of the Jetta; the four door saloon spun off the Golf Mk1 to appeal to buyers wary of the new hatchback concept. With the new Jetta Mk2 Volkswagen saw an opportunity to market the car as a more upmarket proposition, with not only the elongated boot but a new nose with its own grille and square headlamps. The extra size meant that the car could be marketed as a full five seater – but while VW saw it as a premium alternative to the Golf when new, the residuals told a different story. Looking largely pointless next to the Golf meant that Jetta values were lower secondhand, making the primary reason to buy a Jetta used the price saving over an equivalent hatchback model. The Jetta GTi enjoyed a brief renaissance as Sergeant Danny Butterman's wheels in cult film Hot Fuzz, but barring this fillip it's always played second fiddle in image terms to the Gol upon which it was based.

And that image, when the cars were new, had been faultless. Volkswagen buyers, if you ignored the frankly silly advertisements, were sensible people. Generally conservative, Volkswagens were bought by well-heeled professionals looking for a car with a quietly respectable image, good build quality and better residuals. A Golf was never a car bought on a whim, it was always the result of patient, sensible thinking and if you were looking to buy a secondhand one, odds were that it would have every bill and receipt from new.

The primary reason most people wanted to buy a Golf, of course, was the halo effect lent to the range by the GTi variant. With a 1.8 litre fuel injected engine and 16 valves for later models, it was a suitable update to the first generation model which had effectively killed the traditional sports car stone dead. New for

GTi was still the hot hatch everybody wanted.

Jetta took the Golf upmarket into the executive saloon sector.

Golfs were austerely trimmed but well made.

Today, Golfs are popular bases for modified classics.

Jetta was one of the better-executed saloon conversions.

the Mk2 GTi was the option of five door bodywork – the car that killed the sports car off by adding practicality to the mix was set to kill off most of its three door competitors by becoming even more family friendly than ever before. But most families owned more basic Golfs – the Driver model for instance, which offered GTi style with less powerful engines and less lunatic insurance premiums. Even the lowly CL model had its admirers; Volkswagen may not have loaded these cars to the gunwales with kit but they retained the key German attributes of style and solidity. A Golf would last you, and would hold its value to boot. Officially, there was no Mk2 Golf cabrio, the older car holding on until the 1990s alongside the fresher-faced hatchbacks.

Unofficially, many of the changes made in its latter years were intended to better align it with the Mk2, and many consider the late cabrios to be part of the Mk2 family in spirit.

Volkswagen would apply the same formula when it came to replacing the Mk2 Golf as it had when replacing the first generation car in the first place. The formula worked, after all, so there was no reason to change it. Just make the car a bit bigger, a bit softer edged, while keeping the reliability and solidity upon which the Golf had earned its spurs. ∎

	Volkswagen Golf 1.3	Volkswagen Jetta 1.6	Volkswagen Golf GTi	Volkswagen Golf GTi 16v
CAPACITY	1272cc	1595cc	1781cc	1781cc
POWER	54bhp	75bhp	100bhp	139bhp
TORQUE	71lb.ft	92lb.ft	105lb.ft	124lb.ft
TOP SPEED	94mph	100mph	107mph	125mph

A simple and logical dashboard made the Golf easy to drive.

An unlikely hero for the drifting community.

Volvo 300-series

Yes, it was a DAF in drag, but the Volvo 300 series brought Swedish image to the driveways of suburbia.

When you look back at its history, the position the Volvo 300-series enjoys in the classic car scene today appears almost bewildering. Beloved of the classic modifying scene, there are far more 340s and 360s today converted into drift cars than there are restored to concours condition – and not only that, but far more survive in good condition as a result of this than of many of the car's contemporaries. And yet when you look at them on paper it makes sense. They're compact, cheap, and – crucially – rear wheel drive. And as BMW E30s rise ever further out of reach, the dinky Volvo offers the ideal solution for those seeking sideways fun on a budget. These days, it's cool.

And yet when they were new, that couldn't have been much more different. Yes, the Volvo 340 was sold by the same dealerships as the tank-like 240 so beloved of the antiques fraternity, but the Swedes behind the 240 would argue that the 340 was Dutch to them. It had been under development by

Early cars wore 343 or 345 badging, depending on the number of doors.

BODYGUARDS COST LESS THAN ESCORTS.

If you and your family could do with some extra protection on the road, may we offer the services of the 1983 Volvo 340 Hatchback?

If any trouble runs into this bodyguard, it has to contend with a solid steel safety cage and steel bars in the door.

We admit there are a couple of soft spots, namely the front and rear crumple zones.

But paradoxically they add to the strength of the car, by absorbing shocks before they can reach the people inside.

Like all good bodyguards, however, it also helps you avoid trouble.

The servo-assisted brakes provide safe, well-balanced braking.

The rack and pinion steering is both light and precise.

And the Volvo's superior road holding comes from its near-perfect weight distribution. (Like the Porsche 928, the gearbox is over the rear axle.)

Yet despite its tough exterior, the interior of the 340 is remarkably refined.

The fascia is designed to give you perfect access to the controls, with 13 warning lights visible at a glance.

The driver's seat is electrically heated, and both front seats have head restraints.

The boot is carpeted.

And safety belts are fitted to the rear seats.

Now you might imagine that such a stylish bodyguard would come expensive.

In fact, it costs £4,892.

Or to put it another way, £415 cheaper than an Escort.*

THE VOLVO 340 HATCHBACK £4892. www.darrenw.com

Unconvincing saloon added breadth to the range.

DAF as a replacement for the CVT-driven 66 when Volvo bought the company seeking to expand. After a short period of rebadged Volvo 66 models, the would-be DAF 77 was launched under the Volvo 343 moniker. It featured a 1.4 litre four pot borrowed from Renault alongside DAF's signature CVT transmission. Future models would sprout bigger engines, including Volvo's own 2.0 in the

360 – with optional four door saloon or five door hatchback bodywork, and more and more toys. But while Volvo clearly had executive aspirations for its smallest model it's arguably better-remembered as the favourite of the bowls club; the car you bought if you were too well off to slum it in a Metro. Volvo 300s with battered bumpers and scuffed wheels were a common

sight through the 1980s and well into the 1990s, and these cars suffered a long wait bouncing along the bottom level of bangerdom before their rear wheel drive credentials earned them a place in the pantheon of affordable classic greats.

Such a future was unthinkable in the early days of the 300-series, when the car was rear wheel drive purely and simply because

that's what cars were. And if your grandparents turned up at the school gates in a whining CVT Volvo, it was social suicide when compared to the other kids getting into Cortinas and Cavaliers. But the little Volvo wasn't a bad car when viewed for what it was – which in many ways, wasn't even a Volvo. The project had its origin in the cars of Dutch company DAF. Like most small

family car manufacturers, DAF had seen and liked the hatchback layout of VW's Golf and wanted to replicate it, but needed money. A joint venture proposal ultimately led to the purchase of DAF by Volvo and the rebadging of its existing and future models under the Volvo marque – the DAF77 prototype launching as the Volvo 343 and 345. In 1980 your 343DL would have cost you £4375, while the five door 345DL was £4676. Manual versions of both were available by then, retailing at around £220 less in each case. That meant the 300 was aimed squarely against the top half of the VW Golf range, with the Escort and even the Alfasud pitched in a similar ballpark.

The fitment of standard manual gearboxes rendered the 300 more socially tolerable, while from 1983 a new model was introduced that actually made the car much more interesting to the enthusiastic driver. The 360 did not, as its name suggested, have a six cylinder engine – what it had was the 2.0 unit borrowed from the larger 240 in carburetted and injected forms. Between the extra power and the transaxle gearbox, the underpinnings of the 360 meant it became something of an entertaining steer – halfway between a hot hatch and a small executive car in concept and – while offbeat – capable enough to be considered by buyers of both. Four door saloons were added for 1984, to boost the profile of the range and make it more viable as an executive proposition.

But while these cars had the attributes to make them seem like viable competition to the BMW 316, the truth was that the market no more saw these as BMW rivals than the Rover 216 Vitesse – which, at just shy of ten grand in 1987, was not only the same sort of money as a 360GLT but similarly priced to an entry level 316. Both models occupied a weird hinterland of prestigious pretension that marked them as a cut above something like an Escort XR3i, but without really being considered as alternatives to the Germans.

Volvo would adopt a different tactic for its next small family car, the 440 and 460 series. Spun from the platform of the front wheel drive 480ES coupe, the numbering system would now denote whether the car was a four door saloon or five door hatchback. These cars not only failed to attract the British public in the same way as their predecessor had new, but by dint of their front wheel drive platform they never really crossed the boundary from old car to cult classic either. Ultimately that one attribute – the rear wheel drive chassis underpinning a lightweight and compact body – has elevated the 300-series to a status even Volvo never really believed it would reach. ■

	Volvo 340 1.4	Volvo 340 1.7	Volvo 360
CAPACITY	1397cc	1721cc	1986cc
POWER	70bhp	80bhp	115bhp
TORQUE	80lb.ft	96lb.ft	118lb.ft
TOP SPEED	106mph	107mph	112mph

triumph acclaim

The great white hope of the British motor industry was little more than a Honda with Cortina seats

If you were to speak to anybody in the motor trade in the 1980s to find out what they felt the best Austin Rover car was, nine times out of ten you'd hear a single answer. The Triumph Acclaim. But the car that sounded the death knell for the Triumph brand owed much more to Tokyo than to Coventry. It was the first fruit of a joint venture that had been three years in the making; British Leyland had a confusing range of outdated models and very little money to replace them long term. Import quotas set by the EEC on Japanese imports meant that joint ventures and European bases were of benefit to the Japanese motor industry. This led to cars such as the Alfa Romeo Arna – a Nissan Cherry body thrown over the running gear of the Alfasud to make the ultimate in bewildering hybrids; Japanese style and Italian reliability. The benefit of a joint venture with a Japanese manufacturer for BL was that it would remain on an equal footing – it had explored joint ventures with Renault and GM but feared being swamped.

Bullish marketing helped the Acclaim to find its place in the market.

When BL executives flew out to Japan and were presented with the Honda Ballade as a possible basis for a joint venture, they felt it would fit in well alongside the proposed new British Maestro and Montego. Not only would it help to retain former Dolomite buyers but by marketing the Ballade as a more niche Triumph model, it would have less of an impact if British buyers weren't ready to accept a Japanese interloper. If it went down like a lead balloon BL executives could simply write off

Cosmetic changes from the Honda were limited to badging.

Triumph, in a way that would have been commercial suicide for the more mainstream Austin brand. Better still, it could be brought to market ahead of Maestro and Montego, ensuring BL could retain interest from customers as buyers began to feel the Allegro and Marina too long in the tooth.

After all, it was something new to sell even if it wasn't a direct replacement.

Ultimately when it was launched in 1982, the Acclaim was little more than a Ballade finished in European colour schemes and fitted with seats based on those from the Ford Cortina in an effort to make extra space for larger European motorists. But the thing is, throughout the 1970s manufacturers like Datsun had patiently been teaching customers that they could have more spec and better reliability than British manufacturers could offer. Giving British customers the chance to buy what was fundamentally a Japanese car with patriotic badging meant that they could reap the benefits without being seen as selling out to a nation with whom we had recently been at war – exactly the same logic Nissan would later try to exploit by establishing a

Odd proportions, but it was a suitable Dolomite replacement.

Avon would add leather trim or a turbocharger, depending upon your tastes.

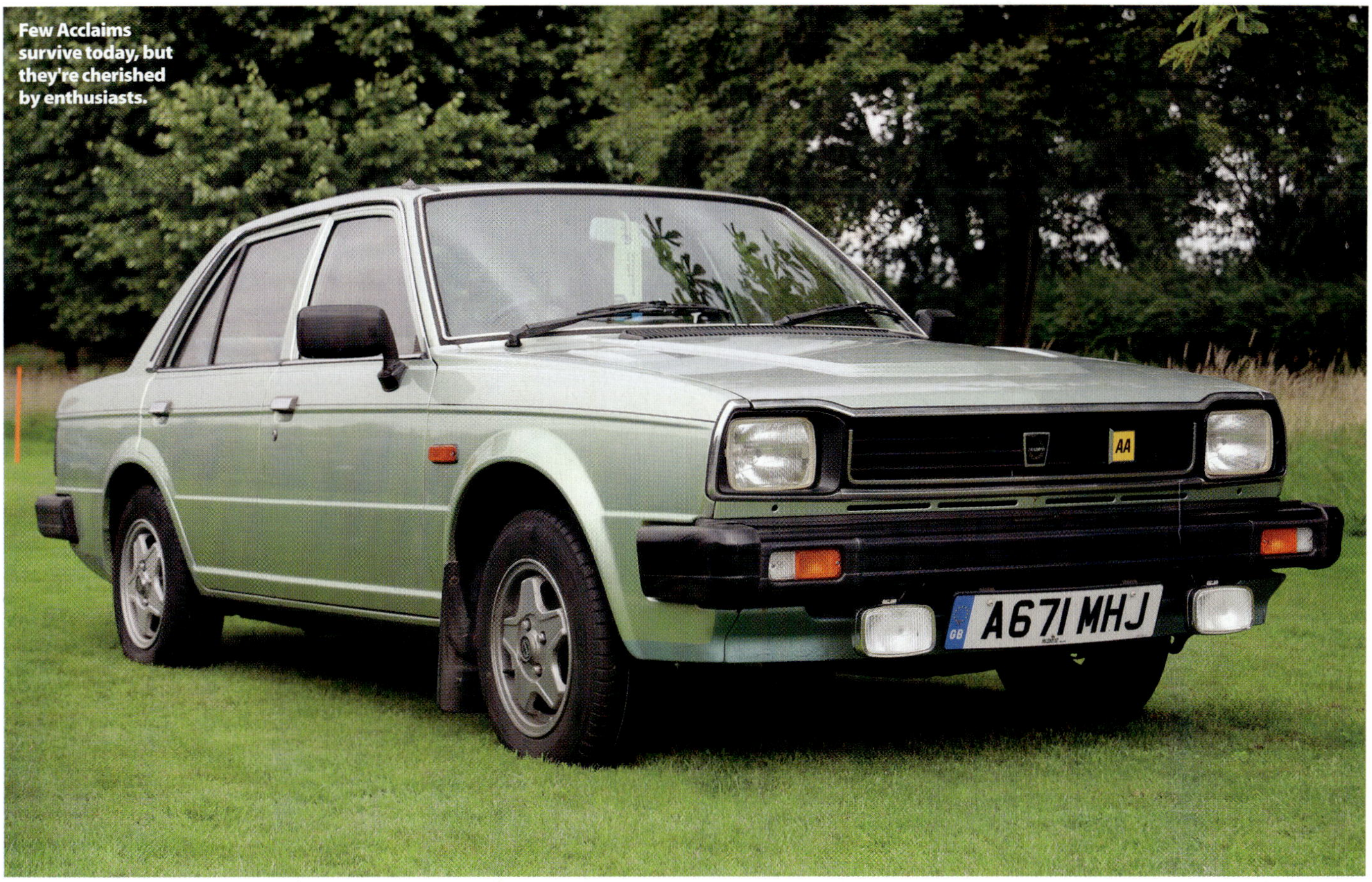

Few Acclaims survive today, but they're cherished by enthusiasts.

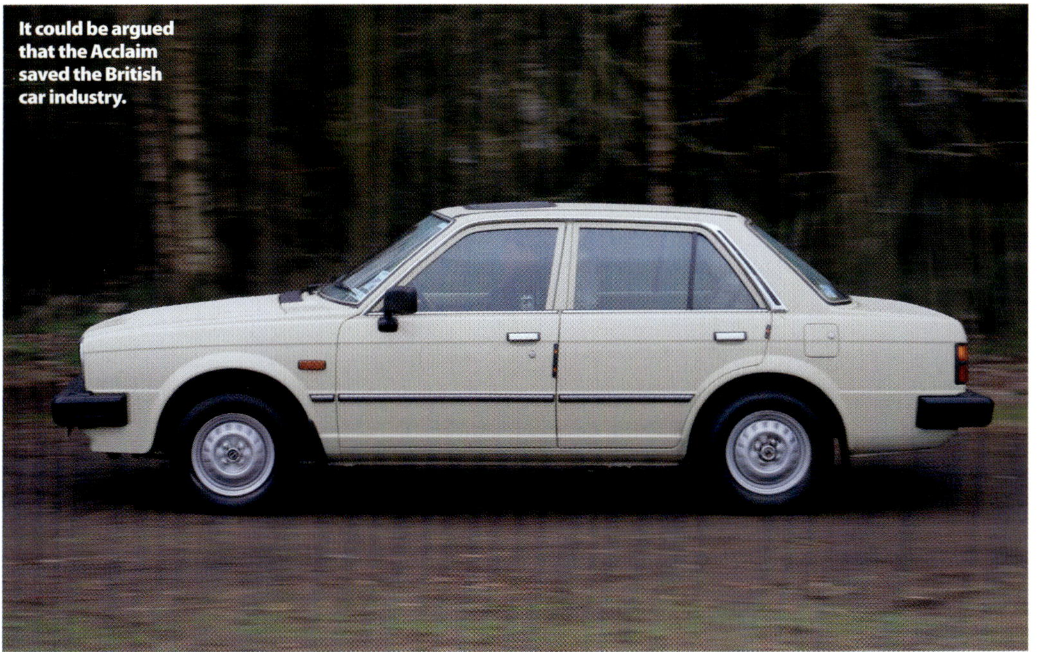

factory in Sunderland. In its first year on sale it reached seventh place in the UK new car sales charts, ahead of established competition including the Volvo 300, the VW Golf and the Nissan Sunny – and not far behind the Vauxhall Astra. The only BL model to sell better was the new and popular Metro supermini. The Maestro leapfrogged it for 1983, but it still stayed in eighth place overall until the Rover 200 series replaced it for 1984. It would be a further three years before that car rejoined the top ten.

The fact that the Acclaim was replaced by a Rover branded car might have been the end of Triumph, and yet it showed that the car had fundamentally done its job. Not only had it given BL a much-needed injection of customer cash, but it served as proof of concept for Honda ahead of its decision to build a shiny new factory in Swindon. For Austin Rover (as it had now become) to risk the premium Rover brand on the next Honda collaboration was a reflection of the way that the Acclaim's clientele had responded to it; and was to foreshadow the way that Austin Rover would develop its new models for the next decade and a half. The Honda cars were to be pitched as premium products sitting above the home-grown equivalents, and it was on this reputation for quality and image that Rover would thrive into the 1990s.

So why is this car, the car that effectively rescued the British motor industry and ensured that thousands of factory workers could stay in work for several decades, not as widely revered as the Mini, the Sierra, even the Cavalier? Why are even the best Acclaims still worth buttons, and why do they appeal to a very niche section of the classic car world? Simply put, small saloons were distinctly passé by the 1980s, and while it enjoyed strong sales to driving schools, blue rinsers, and desperate fleet buyers tied into BL contracts, there was never a sporting variant or a truly luxurious variant to get the pulse racing. Avon Coachworks tried to improve the Acclaim on both counts, offering a two-tone leather trimmed miniature Jaguar and a deep-chinned, alloy-sporting Turbo model, but both were too niche and too expensive to change the public perception of what was still seen as a Japanese car in a bowler hat. Add to this that they rusted for fun; meaning that we had an uncool car that didn't last. Only now, with a handful left, are we recognising them as the greats that they truly were. ■

It could be argued that the Acclaim saved the British car industry.

	Triumph Acclaim
CAPACITY	1335cc
POWER	70bhp
TORQUE	74lb.ft
TOP SPEED	92mph

mini specials

Austin Rover went to a lot of effort to retain interest in its oldest 1980s model

Hanging on in quiet desperation is, as we were once told by a well known song, the English way. And there are few cars that encapsulate this spirit better than the Mini. We've spoken in previous titles in this series about how the Mini was born of spite, designed to drive the influx of post-Suez microcars off the road by offering a small but "real" car as an alternative. It was and will always be one of Britain's great success stories. And yet by the 1980s, it was definitely past its best. Consider that the average car has a lifespan of eight to ten years on sale; by the start of the 1980s the Mini was at 21 and counting.

Austin Rover's attitude was that with fresh trimmings and new model names interest in the Mini could be sustained – and despite the fact that the new Metro meant that the Mini was fundamentally surplus to requirements as well as being labour-intensive to build by 1980s standards, it set about offering a wide array of limited run models in order to try to woo the buying public into a

Alloy wheels and velour trim made the Chelsea a hit.

car that was in many cases as old as its buyers. The Metro was the car aimed at mumsy types and sensible sorts – Austin Rover chose to target the Mini at people who wanted to make a statement with a car that

was very different to any other model on the road. So while the standard range for much of the 1980s consisted of the entry level City E and the less masochistic velour-trimmed Mayfair, the real story for Austin

Rover in the 80s was in the models that lasted mere months at a time.

The first of these, though not the first Mini special edition, was the 25 in 1984. With 3511 of the 5000 built sold in the

Piccadilly was as gold
as Spandau Ballet.

Red Hot and Jet Black were actively targeted at younger drivers.

Both Racing and Flame were meant to be masculine.

If you fancied something a little Ritzy... Austin Rover had you covered.

The RSP Cooper set the tone for Mini into the 1990s.

UK, the Mayfair-based Mini 25 came with standard Silver Leaf paintwork, grey velour seats with map pockets and red piping. The steering wheel and seat belts were red to match the piping, while the front seats bore Mini 25 decals.

The 1980s would also see a second anniversary model; the Mini 30. These were widely considered to be the plushest Minis – cherry red leather for the steering wheel, cut pile carpets to match, half leather, Minilite alloys, chrome grille, bumpers and door handles, and colour coded wheelarches. Most came in Pearlescent Cherry Red – 2000 of the 3000 made - the very first cars built by Rover to come in a Pearlescent colour, as it was a new technology for the company. The remaining 1000 were Pearlescent Black. No coincidence, presumably, that the 30th anniversary traditionally brings gifts of pearls…

"Not everybody gets to live it up in the Ritz" was the strapline of the 1985 Mini Ritz – which offered standard Silver Leaf paintwork and alloy wheels with red, blue and grey velour trim. 2,200 were built, after which Austin Rover launched the Chelsea. Broadly speaking the Chelsea was a Flame Red Ritz with opening rear windows, trying to evoke the 1960s and appeal to yuppies with the line "from flower power to power, flower". Yes, we're cringing too. "Another glittering West End production" came next in the shape of the 1986 Piccadilly – with a Cashmere Gold body, Caramel interior and unique three tone brown, cream and claret seats. Keeping the alloys, chrome bits and opening windows of the Chelsea, it was a shining example of the appeal a colour scheme could bestow. The last of the 1980s London themed cars was the 1987 Park Lane; black with black trim and beige velvet it was arguably the most muted of the lot, though the chromework and alloys ensured it kept an air of class. Originally there was to be a Mini Wimbledon, but the all-white car launched at the 1987 French Open would be sold as the Advantage.

A cassette of soul and chart hits and a free Sony Walkman were the key attractions for the Red Hot and Jet Black, unveiled in 1988 and targeted toward the bright young things who loved the nightlife. The Red Hot was supposed to be passionate, the Jet Black deeply cool – even though in both cases you were basically buying a Mini City with Mayfair wheeltrims, velour trim and some snazzy stripes.

For 1989, Rover got sexist with models specific to the genders. The Racing and Flame were the cars for the boys; the Sky and Rose for the girls. "At last, the Sixties" read the advertising copy for this quarter – all of which came with white wheel trims. The Racing was BRG with a white roof and the Flame Flame Red with a white roof, evoking the Mini's sporting side. The Sky and Rose were both finished in White Diamond – their colour coding was saved for the roofs, with the Sky having a pastel blue finish and the Rose a pastel pink top.

Arguably the most special Mini special edition of the lot, though, would appear right at the start of the following decade. The work of Rover Special Products, who shoehorned a Metro 1.3 engine under the bonnet and shod it with Minilite alloys, the new Mini Cooper of 1990 set the tone for the way Rover would market the car through the 1990s. The Mini would shift from city car to fashion statement with larger engines, fuel injection and plusher trim as time went by – a die that was cast by the myriad specials of the 1980s. ∎

Production models owed a debt to the revival led by 1980s special editions.

	Mini (special editions)
CAPACITY	998cc
POWER	40bhp
TORQUE	51lb.ft
TOP SPEED	81mph

The Vauxhall Nova was beloved of boy racers everywhere.

slower sellers – compact cars

Škoda pricing was no joke.

We don't have space to give every family classic its own section in this title. Here are some of the best of the rest in the compact sector.

The Cold War might have reached its height in the 1980s, but the roads of Britain were still filled with plenty of models from behind the Iron Curtain. Cars like the Škoda Estelle; which was the butt of many a joke for its backward design principles. But the engine slung out over the back wheels, iron head and aluminium block made for a car with entertaining handling – and in Rapid coupe form it looked a little bit like the baby 911 it handled like. But both Škoda and Russian sister Lada had new and shiny front wheel drive hatchbacks for the 1980s, ready to engage in the post glasnost age of perestroika. Lada launched its

new car first; the Samara of 1984, known as the Sputnik back in the Motherland. A three and five door hatchback range, the Samara was supposed to look up to the minute against rivals such as the Volvo 340, Ford Escort and Vauxhall Astra. And when compared with Lada's previous efforts, the Samara did indeed look up to date – it was clean, crisp and wedge-shapes, albeit a little less sharp than the Western competition and with cheaper looking plastics. But from its UK launch in 1988, prices began at just £4295 – an Escort 1.3 competitor for less than the most basic Citroën AX, and it wasn't the same warmed over 1960s fodder we'd come to expect of the Soviet Union. It was the same money as

Nissan Micra was faultlessly reliable. Shame it rusted...

the FSO Polonez, for instance, and that car didn't even have a folding rear seat. The only Soviet car of the era which made the Samara feel like a low rent option was the Škoda Favorit of the following year – the last Škoda to be developed without significant Volkswagen input and the most advanced of all the Eastern Bloc specials.

Priced between £5000 and £5700 it might have been cheaper than the Austin Metro but it was a well-conceived car for those on a budget. It was good enough to form the basis of the Felicia – the small Škoda for the 1990s, which had to reflect well on all the shiny new VW money being pumped into the Czech car maker.

But it wasn't all about the Soviets down at the sharp end – because both Western Europe and Japan offered small cars we all remember to boot. When we spoke of the Triumph Acclaim we mentioned another joint venture between a European and Italian company – the oft-derided Alfa Romeo ARNA. While its easy to mock the car for getting the mix wrong – Japanese style and Italian reliability – the truth was that it had to be this way round to satisfy the need to sidestep EEC regulations. It had to be built in Italy using bits from Japan, melded in the Arna's case with the drivetrain of the Alfasud. And while it looked undeniably

The Citroën AX made the Peugeot 205 look frumpy, but was never as popular as its sister.

Alfa Romeo Arna blended Nissan style with Alfa Romeo reliability. Er...

Japanese, it drove like an Italian thoroughbred. It was always a rare sight in the UK, but it was one of the decade's best hidden secrets. After all, it looked just like a Nissan.

Not that that was necessarily a bad thing – because right when it was transitioning from Datsun to Nissan the company unveiled its smallest offering. The Micra – launched in K10 guide – was the darling of driving schools everywhere. If you learned to drive in the 1980s in anything but a Metro, odds are it was a Nissan Micra. And why not? Japanese reliability and longevity made it the perfect companion for a succession of drivers set on exploding the clutch or kerbing the wheels. And what would all those new motorists want once they passed their tests? Well, a big chunk of them would have started to drive the car in which they passed their tests. Not strictly a family car, but you can bet that Mum or Dad would have commandeered it if their own wheels had broken down.

For younger motorists looking for a dose of style, there was the Citroën AX – a car which not only offered entertaining Peugeot 205-based handling , but offered its own alternative to the 205GTi with more youth-friendly insurance premiums. Many motoring journalists of the era believe the Citroën AX

GT to be the ultimate drivers' car, as it melded the same 205 cornering prowess and lift off oversteer with a rortier-sounding carburetted 1.4 lump shared with the 205XS, and lighter weight to boot. Like the 205 though, the hairy model might have been the headline but it was the small petrols and super-efficient diesels that really stole the show. You could have a little, insurance friendly car that cost buttons to run, but rode

and handled like a much more expensive model.

These were the cars that showed the Ford Fiesta and Vauxhall Nova up for what they were – worthy small cars perhaps, and with plenty of dealers to keep them going, but by and large unimaginative. Ford and Vauxhall capitalised on the ability to sell cars on every street corner to flood the market with Fiestas and Novas, and the odds are that if your dad had a Sierra or Granada

your mum would have a Fiesta from the same dealer – likewise, Cavalier dad would have bought a Nova for Mum. What they had in ease of purchase and ownership, they lost in a lack of imagination. And while Vauxhall at least offered the Nova in a wide range of body styles from the mumsy five door hatch to the geriatric two door saloon, the Fiesta was still stuck with a three-door only range until the launch of the Mk3 at the end of the decade. ∎

Boy racers left the booted Novas to the blue rinse brigade.

Enjoy one of our many titles today!

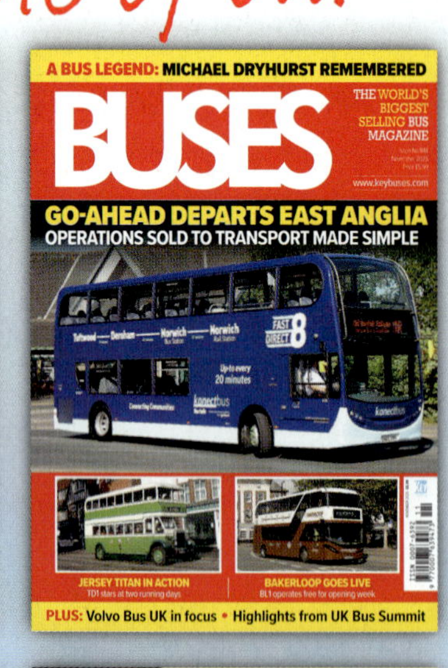

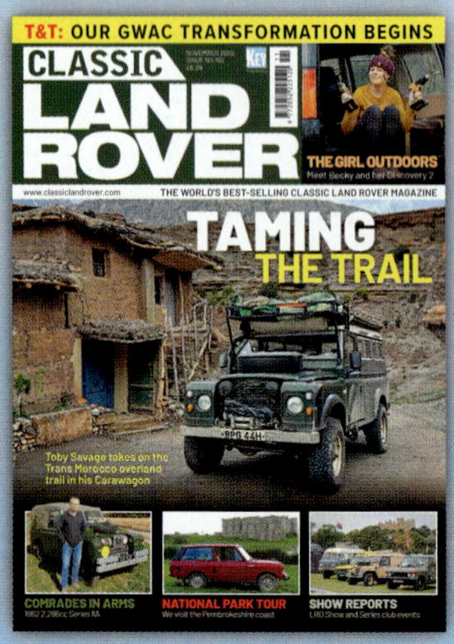

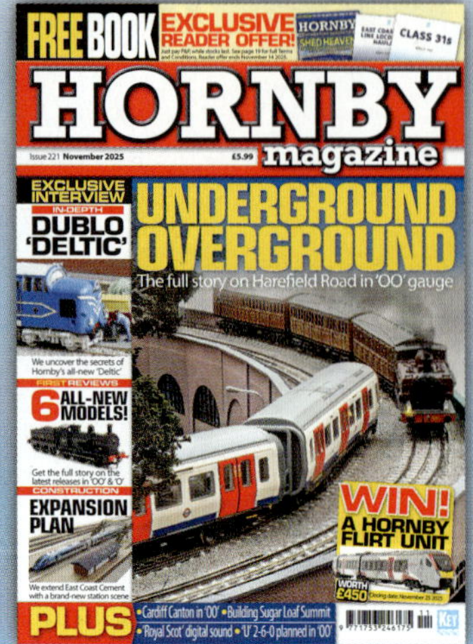

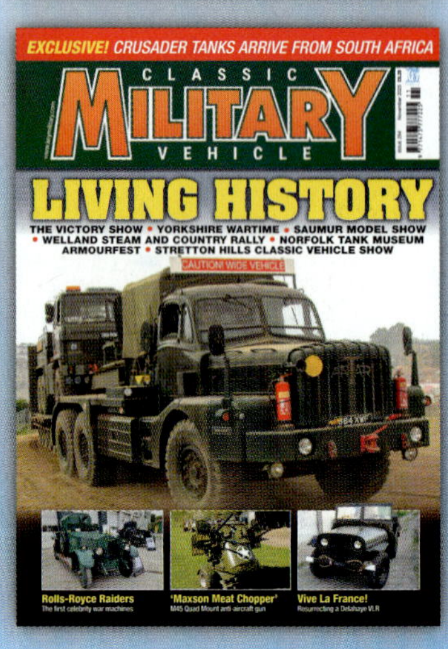

Ford Sierra

The darling of the company car sector perhaps, but the Sierra was very nearly Ford's biggest mis-step.

For a manufacturer so adored by so many, Ford has dropped some real clangers in its time. The infamous case of the Pinto was one of the worst, where Ford calculated that negligent death payouts would be cheaper than a recall and redesign of a part that added less than a dollar to the overall cost price. The Edsel fiasco, where a whole new marque was launched without proper market research into its name or positioning and which left buyers confused as to whether it was meant to be better or worse than a Mercury. The Mk5 Escort, a car so distinctly average it felt as if Ford knew the buying public would buy any old rubbish with a blue oval. And then there was the Sierra. Yes, the Sierra, darling of so many fleet buyers and families growing up – the Sierra could well have been among the biggest mistakes of the lot. Because what we are all too willing to forget with hindsight is that there was a very pregnant pause after the Sierra was launched before the public really embraced the car, and arguably it took until its first

The shape of things to come, but it terrified the fleet market.

facelift for people truly to accept the new design.

When the Sierra was launched in 1982, the public were utterly nonplussed. They were used to this sort of swoopy aero madness from companies such as Citroën, but to be shown a jelly mould and told that this was the new Cortina was a step many simply weren't willing to take. The Cortina had been safe, dull, a bit unimaginative. It was the perfect riposte to cars like the Princess or some of those deeply suspicious new EEC-friendly imports from the continent, a plain and simple three box, rear wheel drive saloon car for people who wanted no nonsense transport. The Sierra looked like a concept car. Indeed, we'd been given a preview of it with the 1981 Probe III concept; a Sierra with swoopy bumpers and wheel spats. And Mr Average, who'd passed by the Princess and bought himself a Cortina,

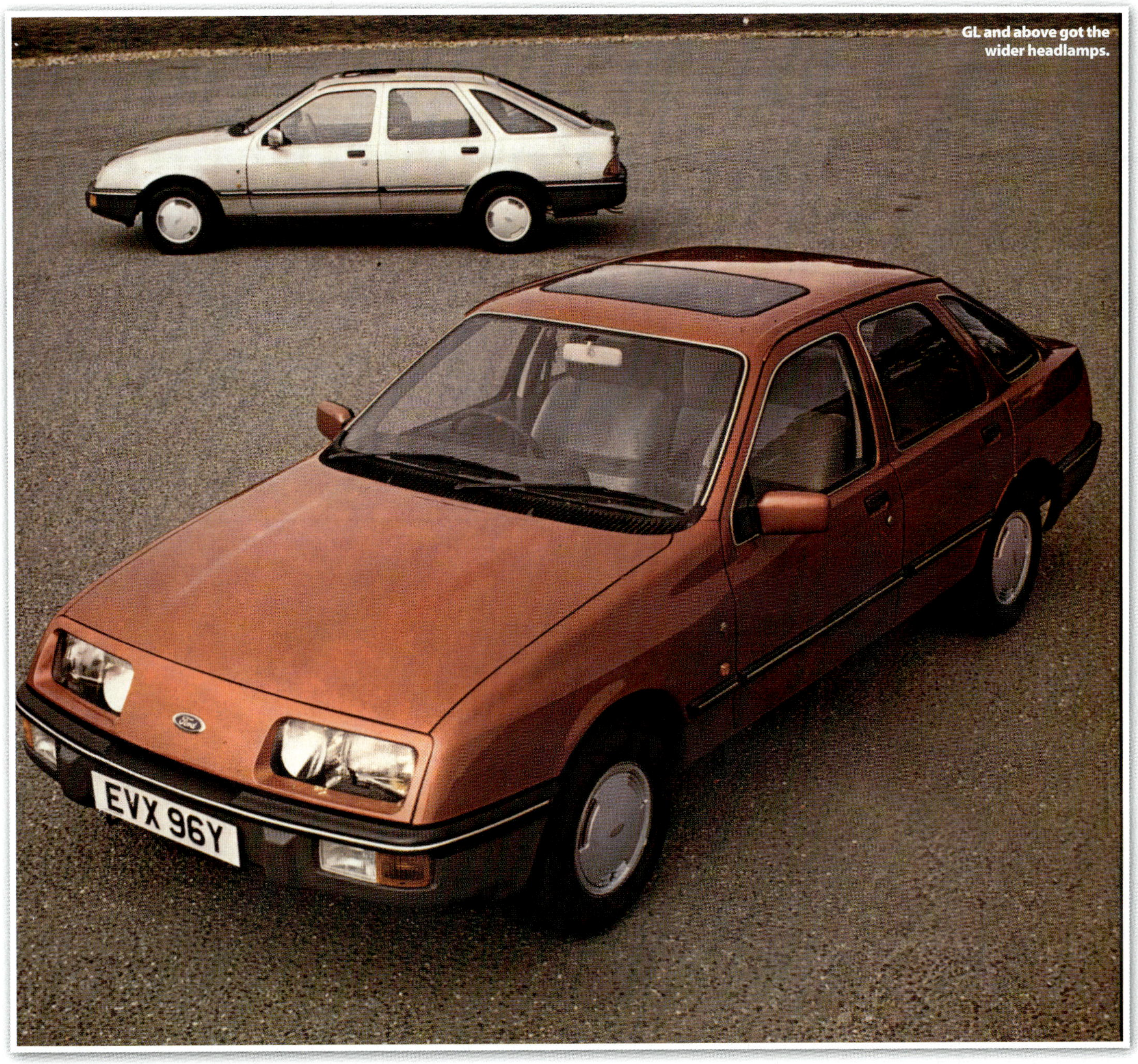
GL and above got the wider headlamps.

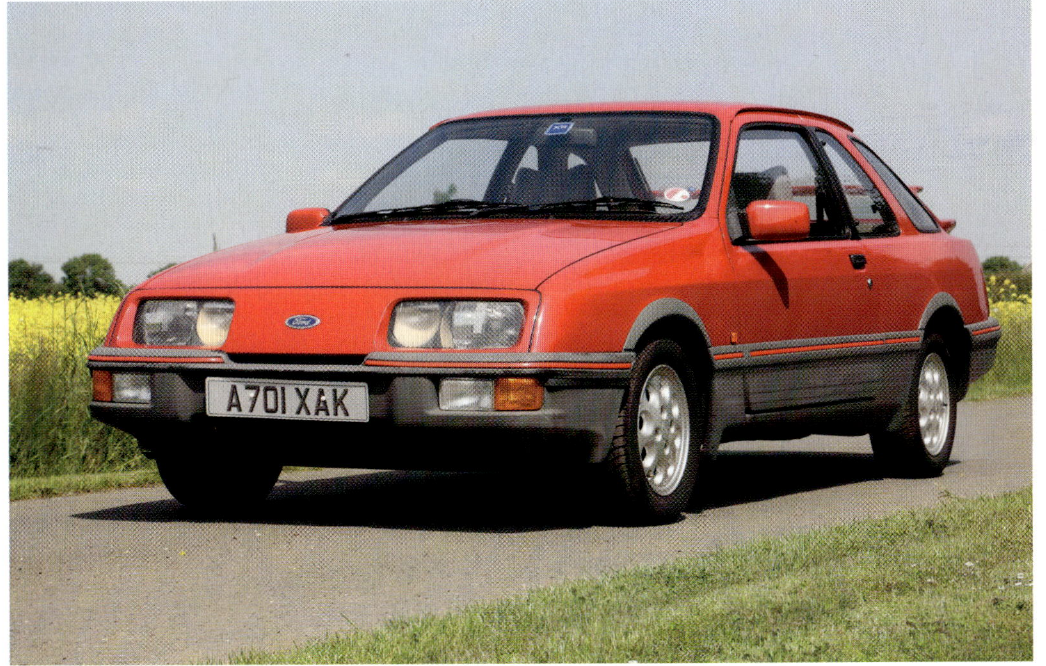

XR4i was marketed as a Capri replacement, with styling inspired by the Porsche 928. Yes, really.

was having none of it. Never mind that under the skin it was all deeply conventional Cortina-based fare, buyers flocked instead to the more advanced front wheel drive Vauxhall Cavalier in the Sierra's early years simply because it looked so much more palatable.

What was even worse was that this car had delusions of grandeur – Ford launched a separate three door hatchback body, fitted the 2.8i engine, called it an XR4i and told buyers to treat it as a replacement for the Capri. The fact that it was faster then the Capri and more up to date underneath meant nothing – this was the car that wanted to usurp the hero.

Where the Sierra redeemed itself though was in the development of a new hero. Ford wanted a car to enter into touring car competitions – and

Wings and skirts identfied the Sierra that everybody wanted - the Cosworth, seen here in RS500 form.

Cosworth had just developed the right engine for the job. A twin cam development of the Pinto, turbocharged and offering just over 200bhp in production form. When Ford shoehorned it into a three door Sierra shell and badged it Sierra RS, it created a legend.

Five years after the launch of the Sierra, Ford capitulated – it launched a saloon variant. The new car had a submodel name, in a bid to differentiate it from the hatchback variants and allow Ford to argue that it met a different range need in the manner of the Orion, but the truth was obvious – fleet buyers of the very last Cortinas hadn't returned in 1985 for a Sierra, and Ford was keen to win them back. Helpfully, the new Sapphire shell was significantly stiffer even than the three door hatchback, making it an obvious choice for the next iteration of the Cosworth bahnstormer. The Sapphire Cosworth – and subsequent Sapphire Cosworth 4x4, subtly shifted the car's market position, targeting the executive market and pitching as alternative transport for the family man who had done well. In 1988, a Sapphire Cosworth would set you back £20250 – making it a viable alternative on company car lists for directors entitled to Scorpios or a left field private buyer option instead of an entry level Jag.

But for every schoolboy desperate for his dad to bring home a Cossie, there was a kid whose dad had a nice sensible 1.6L or 2.0GL – and these were the cars upon which the Sierra built its fortune. Simple,

Estate managed to look much swoopier than it was, courtesy of unique rear doors and a clamshell tailgate.

Facelift smoothed out the Sierra shape even further.

Unorthodox dash angled toward the driver to create a cockpit feel. Inside, there was seating for five.

The last Cosworths were based on the four door Sapphire shell.

honest, dependable transport underneath that futuristic body, and by the time the nation's fleet managers had cottoned on it was hard to find a motorway service station car park with fewer than 15 Sierras at any given time. Top of the heap was the Ghia, unless you were lucky enough to get the 1989 2000E. The model was conceived as a halo model to preview Ford's new twin cam four, and added to Ghia spec with standard leather, two tone paint and alloy wheels.

Ford would replace the Sierra with the Mondeo for 1993 – and with this car, it got it right. Modern yet subtle styling hiding front wheel drive and a chassis that got the press raving made for a package that people were proud to own – against which, the Sierra would look distinctly old hat. Ford had learned from its mistake – and wouldn't look to shake up quite such a conservative market sector again. ∎

	Ford Sierra 1.6	Ford Sierra 2.0i	Ford Sierra 2.3	Ford Sierra XR4	Ford Sierra RS Cosworth
CAPACITY	1594cc	1993cc	2294cc	2792cc	1993cc
POWER	75bhp	115bhp	114bhp	150bhp	204bhp
TORQUE	88lb.ft	118lb.ft	130lb.ft	130lb.ft	205lb.ft
TOP SPEED	104mph	117mph	115mph	125mph	143mph

nissan bluebird

The start of a real revolution – the Bluebird was the first Japanese-branded car to be built in Britain

Japanese import quotas of the early 1980s into the EEC led to some unexpected half-breeds – cars that combined Japanese technology with European branding and absolutely weren't attempts to circumnavigate the quotas by claiming that the cars were European. Oh no, manufacturers wouldn't do that. We had the Triumph Acclaim, which was a Cortina-seated Honda with British paint colours and trim. In Italy, there was the Alfa Romeo Arna – a project intended to replace the Alfasud with a car that employed all the reliability of an Alfa Romeo and design flair of a Datsun Cherry.

But the Arna project itself wasn't enough for Nissan. Company bosses were exploring agreements to establish a manufacturing base within the EEC – somewhere that the company could build more than one model in time, and where the models built didn't also have to fit in with the plans of a rival manufacturer. And it was Britain's government with which it signed an agreement in 1984 to bring employment to the North

East with a proposal to build a 799 acre plant in Sunderland, Tyne and Wear. The first fruit of the factory, which now (sadly) produces the Juke, was the Bluebird of 1986. The T12 Bluebird was effectively a rebadged and locally manufactured variant of the Nissan Violet, built using componentry sourced from Japan as a remote assembly plant. Helpfully, this ensured that quotas of imported vehicles could be circumvented. As far as Europe was concerned, the Bluebird was as British as a Montego.

And while the Nissan Bluebird may not have been the most interesting car in the world, it was a perfectly capable vehicle. They went fairly well, steered nicely and rode perfectly acceptably, the four door and five door bodies were spacious,

Styling was simple, but inoffensive.

and they were sufficiently different to appear interesting on driveways and company fleets when surrounded by endless Cavaliers and Sierras. Nissan included helpful touches for the fleet user such as a second tripmeter, to enable people to differentiate between personal and business mileage, while hard wearing seat trim endeared it to those whose daily grind included pounding the motorways of Britain from rush hour to contraflow. These factors, plus Japanese reliability, also endeared it to minicab drivers – with the exception of the Hyundai Stellar, there was no better value alternative for private hire drivers than a second-hand T12.

The Bluebird enjoyed a solid reputation in Britain for a number of reasons. Datsun had made considerable waves in Britain during the 1970s, when it offered cars that came at an attractive price with all the options as standard. Cars that – while they rusted just as well as ours did – stood a chance of starting in winter. Models like the Sunny 120Y had also been

a hit simply because because they were available, unlike home-grown models from British Leyland where your new car's delivery date depended very much on whether Derek Robinson had had a good enough breakfast not to fancy standing on a picket line in the rain. That reputation preceded the Bluebird and ensured that buyers flocked to showrooms – while the aversion of some sectors of society to buying a Japanese car was tempered by the knowledge that it had been put together by hardy Brits on Wearside. It wasn't usually the sort of car your dad would buy – more the sensible car your grandad might choose upon retirement in the knowledge It would see him out if cared for. You could stick all the turbochargers, leather seats or Executive badges you liked onto the Bluebird, it was never really an aspirational family car – more a solid, worthy machine bought for its many sensible qualities. And much as their image might have suggested, they lasted. We know of at least two Bluebirds still in regular use near the home of the author of this title – no Montegos, no Sierras, no Cavaliers. And they're evidently cared-for but used, they're not show cars. For an ordinary family saloon still to be doing its job day in, day out after almost forty years is a remarkable achievement and one that speaks of the staying power of the model.

Thatcher approved of the jobs Bluebird brought.

Bluebird was plush, but looked cheap next to Cavalier.

From July 1986, all Bluebird saloons were built in Britain while the hatchbacks were still imported from Japan. Estate models were always imported, but these were based on the older U11 platform rather than the T12 we remember most fondly. From 1987 and the start of hatchback production in Sunderland, only British T12 Bluebirds were available in the UK – and they enjoyed an almost invidious position as far as other manufacturers went. Being built in the UK, the T12 Bluebird was seen as a European vehicle and was thus not subjected to the same quotas as other Nissans. This meant it could be exported to mainland Europe – meaning more production and even more work for the British teams behind them. A third shift was approved from 1987, with Bluebirds produced for the UK and mainland Europe around the clock.

The next car to be built at Sunderland, the Nissan Primera, would not only be constructed here but made in Britain in its entirety. It would pick up where the Bluebird left off, offering reliability and competency into the 1990s. Unlike the Bluebird that it replaced, it also offered buyers a little style. ∎

	Nissan Bluebird 1.6	Nissan Bluebird 2.0	Nissan Bluebird Turbo
CAPACITY	1598cc	1973cc	1809cc
POWER	82bhp	105bhp	135bhp
TORQUE	98lb.ft	120lb.ft	121lb.ft
TOP SPEED	95mph	102mph	120mph

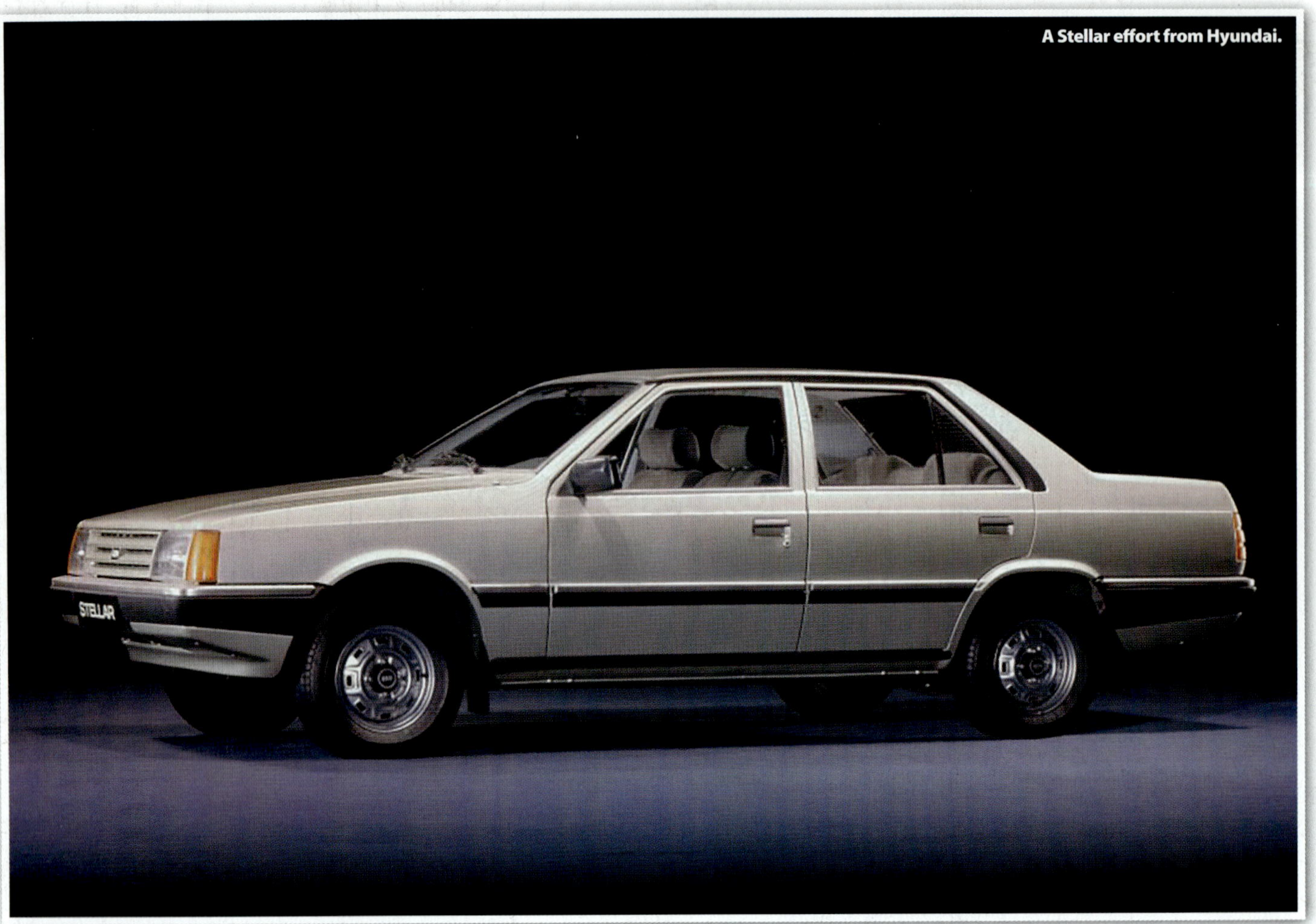

A Stellar effort from Hyundai.

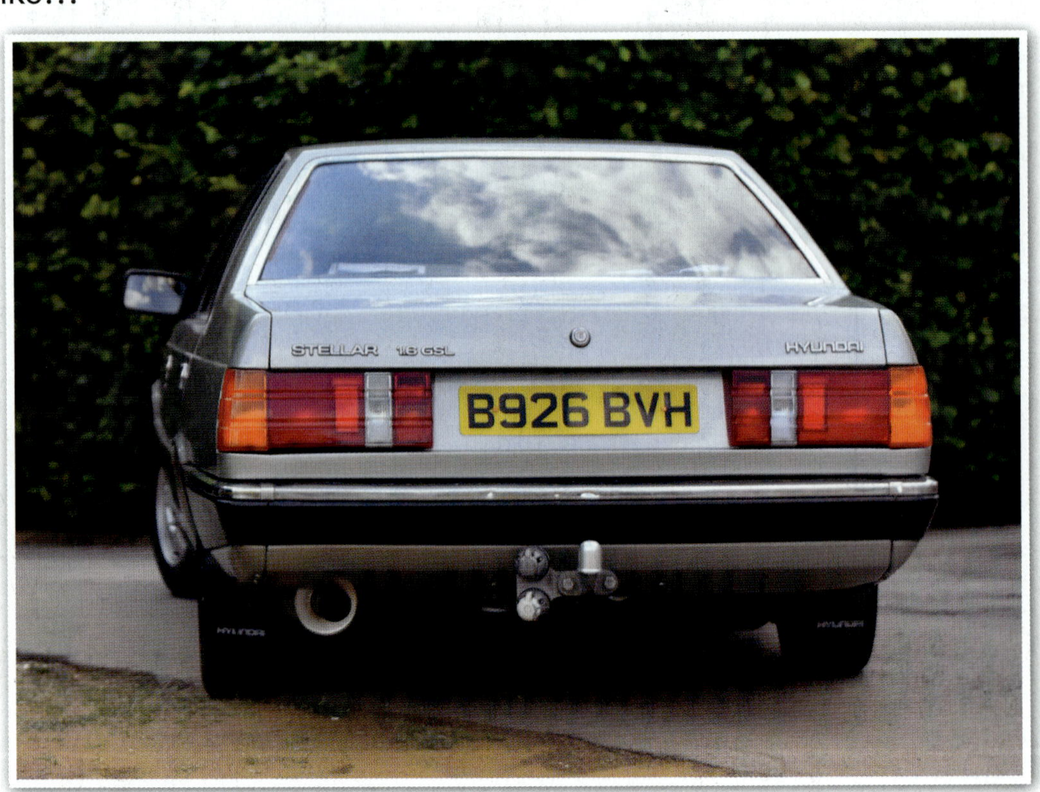

hyundai stellar

Ford cocked up with the Sierra, but there was a car to clean up the mess. Step forward, the unofficial Cortina Mk6…

Let's be completely honest here. The vast majority of people reading this will not have had a Hyundai Stellar. They won't have had family member who owned one. But almost everybody of a certain generation will have ridden in one, even if they didn't remember it. Because for several years there was no finer minicab than the Stellar, which married proven Ford Cortina-inspired underpinnings with the reliability of Mitsubishi-sourced engines. As someone growing up in the 1980s, the back seat of a Stellar would have been a very familiar spot. Maybe you had your first drunken fumble on the back seat on the way back to your girlfriend's flat. Maybe it was the taxi booked to take you to school. Or maybe it took you to the station to go and have your first proper job interview. At the end of every drunken

Advertising made it plain
that Hyundai was gunning for
disgruntled Cortina buyers.

We saw the successor to the Cortina in a different mould.

Many people mourned the passing of the much loved Cortina.

And, alas, they were not overjoyed with its replacement, the Sierra.

"A jelly mould" some have even been heard to cry.

Now at last a serious successor has arrived.

The new Stellar 1.6 from Hyundai the company that built Cortinas in the Far East. A car that makes other 1.6 saloons pale in comparison.

At almost 2 inches longer and wider it makes a Cavalier look small.

With 5 speed gearbox, central locking, electric windows, headlamp washers, alloy wheels, and stereo radio/cassette the 1.6 GSL makes the nearest priced Sierra look rather basic.

At £4,500 on the road the 1.6 L even makes an Escort look expensive.

'Phone Teledata 01-200 0200 for a brochure and the name and address of your nearest dealer. **HYUNDAI**

The new Stellar 1.6. £4,500 to £5,500 on the road.

night in the pub or flight home from Alicante there would always be a Stellar waiting for you, engine ticking over, meter running.

And if we're honest, the back seat is probably the best place from which to enjoy the Stellar. Because unlike so many manufacturers, Hyundai did not inject its cars with passion at the factory. Instead, it developed cars to meet a need. George Turnbull, the mind behind the Morris Marina, had been instrumental in the development of Hyundai's first truly independent model – the Pony – and his lead was one that Hyundai followed when Ford stopped offering them knock-down Cortina kits. Simply put; source engines from Mitsubishi and get Giugiaro to style a new body. The Stellar looked like a Mk6 Cortina might have looked, which endeared it to British buyers frightened off by the aero styling of the new Sierra. In a forward thinking new world of front wheel drive and aerodynamics, the Stellar was defiantly retrograde, with rear wheel drive and a three box

body allowing buyers to rest comfortably in a package that had changed little in concept since the 1950s. The sense that buyers were getting the Cortina they really wanted and the Fiesta 950L-rivalling price of the entry level Stellar 1.6L made it the perfect mode of transport for people who needed space, simplicity and affordable running costs.

So what if it wasn't cool? Buyers knew what they were getting – which on the range topping GSL meant that for Orion 1.3L money they could have crushed velour seating, electric windows and central locking as standard – alongside a 12 month warranty with unlimited mileage. Plus, as Britain's number one least desirable car to thieves for several years in a row, insurance premiums were about as cheap as the servicing bills. And as long as you stayed on top of servicing – and often, even if you didn't – those Mitsubishi mechanicals meant that your Stellar wouldn't break the bank to own either. Even as the cars vanished from the roads, parts remained both inexpensive and

readily available. It might have been the automotive equivalent of a pair of Bensonshoe loafers, but the only way A to B could be cheaper is if you relied upon Shanks' pony. And it really wasn't that bad. Yes, we did say the back seat was the best seat, but that's not to say the Stellar didn't drive okay. Uninspiring perhaps, dull, but perfectly competent and the optional power steering made it one of the easier cars of its price to drive to boot.

Of course, being a cheap car when new from a largely unknown manufacturer, the Stellar was hardly a stellar performer on the secondhand market. By the end of the 1990s a ten year old Stellar was valued at just £400, even with low miles and in good condition. But that just meant that the buyer demographic changed from people wanting a cheap car to people wanting a nice one – and for the people buying a Stellar as

a used car, it must have seemed like a Rolls-Royce. Yes, we're serious. Because let's be honest here. If all your parents could afford in the mid to late 1990s was a tired Marina or a dog eared old Polo, the Stellar was not only a much more reliable prospect but a far more modern and comfortable one too. Not only that, but here was a car that suited newly self-employed minicab drivers perfectly, being modern enough to meet plating

requirements but cheap enough to justify when getting started. You'd spend twice as much even for a 2CV of the same age, and that couldn't manage a quick airport run before the school run.

Hyundai replaced the Stellar in the UK with two models – the smaller Lantra was intended as a direct replacement, while the larger and slightly more upmarket Sonata was the car that most Stellar owners found themselves considering as a replacement. While the Stellar itself hadn't been a runaway success in Britain, the Lantra and Sonata found even fewer buyers in Britain. The momentum the Stellar managed to maintain courtesy of its Cortina links and the Sierra's poor start simply didn't carry over to anodyne and pseudo—Japanese designs of the early 1990s, with buyers looking for cars of that ilk choosing to buy Japanese models instead. ■

Stellar was well-equipped and comfortable for the money.

	Hyundai Stellar
CAPACITY	1597cc
POWER	72bhp
TORQUE	101lb.ft
TOP SPEED	95mph

vauxhall cavalier mk2

The car that got the rep formula so right, it outdid Ford.

Oh how Vauxhall must have laughed. The follow-up to its first Cavalier – which had been a runaway success – was not without risk. In a super conservative marketplace used to the simplicity of rear wheel drive and the ease of access to Ford dealers, going up against the established market leader with something new was a ballsy strategy. The Mk2 Cavalier was that car – it still looked like the older car, but under the skin it boasted new and economical engines along with front wheel drive. But Vauxhall – and its parent company General Motors – needn't have been worried. Because in 1981 the Cavalier looked fresh and sharp, while the Cortina was basically the same car Ford had launched in 1977 as the MkIV with little but a light facelift to drag it kicking and screaming into the 1980s.

Vauxhall knew there would be a new Ford coming, and that this was likely to regain the top spot in the company car sector – but nobody was expecting what Ford had planned. It replaced the conservative Cortina with the swish new Sierra – whose

Range-topper at launch was the GLS.

Cosmetic differences between the Cavalier and Open Ascona were by now limited to badging.

Estates used Holden bodyshells and were actually shorter than the saloons.

boldly aerodynamic appearance endeared it to approximately none of the Cortina's loyal customers. While the Sierra's underpinnings differed little from those of the old model, the scary swoopy shell meant that traditional fleet managers were drawn back in the direction of Luton. Yes, the Cavalier was a hatchback as well, but it didn't look like it had beamed down from the moon – and there was a sensible saloon variant for buyers longing for a new Cortina. Early saloons could even be had in two door form, though sales never rose above a handful and after two years all Cavalier saloons in the UK became four door only models. It took a couple of years to arrive in the UK, but there was even an estate – developed in Australia where the car was marketed as the Holden Camira, and with rear bodywork imported into the UK direct from the Holden factory. The estate was always a slow seller though at 7% of total production – not as bad as the two-door saloon which was dropped just two years into production, but bad enough to warrant no effort being put into development of a Cavalier Mk3 estate variant.

We feel it necessary to issue a warning to Cavalier SRi drivers.

As you wait at the lights, don't forget the potential that's ticking over beneath the bonnet.

The 1.8 litre engine, with Bosch LE Jetronic fuel-injection, produces 115 bhp. Off the line it takes just 9.4 seconds to reach 60 mph.

On a foreign motorway it will power on to over 114 mph, and that's in fourth gear. Fifth is an overdrive which helps the SRi return 36.7 mpg at a constant 75 mph.

The mileage is eked out even further by 'fuel cut-off'. This stops the flow of petrol when the accelerator is released above 1,200 rpm.

But that's enough on technical merit. Now consider style and presentation.

Outside, it sports an aerodynamic rear spoiler. Plus 195/60 HR ultra low-profile tyres on alloy wheels.

Inside, it features Recaro seats; just as much a measure of performance as the comprehensive bank of instruments.

Both hatchback and saloon versions of the SRi have tinted glass, electrically operated and heated door mirrors and a radio/stereo cassette with four speakers.

So far so good on paper. But the acid test is on the road.

And who better to pass judgement than the motoring experts.

"Excellent front-wheel drive handling, good gearchange and driving position, firm braking characteristics combine to produce a satisfying driver's car." So said 'Motor'.

'Autosport' were just as complimentary about the SRi: "...combines the characteristics of a quiet and refined family saloon and a fast sports car remarkably successfully."

So all that remains is to remind you that when you take a test drive, take it easy.

VAUXHALL CAVALIER SRi.

Better. By Design.

PERFORMANCE FIGURES ARE FROM 'MOTOR' MAGAZINE. ROAD TEST QUOTES FROM 'MOTOR': JANUARY 9TH, 1983 AND 'AUTOSPORT': APRIL 7TH, 1983. SRi SALOON COSTS £7,127; SRi HATCH NUMBER PLATES ARE EXTRA. DOT FUEL CONSUMPTION TESTS MPG (LITRES/100KM) FOR SRi HATCH AND SALOON COSTS £7,364 (2-COAT METALLIC PAINT AND SUNROOF ARE EXTRA COST OPTION). PRICES, WHICH ARE CORRECT AT TIME OF GOING TO PRESS, INCLUDE CAR TAX AND VAT. DELIVERY AND (5-SPEED MANUAL): URBAN CYCLE: 25.7 (11.0), CONSTANT 56 MPH: 48.7 (5.8), CONSTANT 75 MPH: 36.7 (7.7).

Clever advertising hid a very capable car - late Cavalier SRis offered up to 130bhp.

There was no new Cavalier coupe – GM continuing to sell the old model under Opel Manta badging instead – but for 1984 there was a convertible variant that enjoyed celebrity patronage.

Harry Enfield was a proud owner of the car he saw as a cut-price 3-series cabrio. Well – he was a comedian. But while the Cavalier never had quite the kudos of a BMW it was still seen as slightly premium no matter what the flavour. All Cavaliers, clearly, shared all but their badging with the Opel Ascona – and Opel was cool; it made the Manta and the Monza, and it was German just like those interesting BMWs and Audis. While the image of the Vauxhall brand was decidedly Luton, the cars themselves could pass for German – especially in sporting specs with blacked out

Topless fun was even enjoyed by celebrities - Harry Enfield loved his Cavalier convertible.

Comfortable interiors - and better handling than the Sierra.

window frames. A Cavalier SR may not have been as hairy as a Sierra XR4i, but it looked every bit as purposeful as a BMW 320 and at £5867, it was almost two grand cheaper.

Vauxhall gained an advantage in Britain over rivals by – initially – offering just 1.6 litre Cavaliers as high end models, and enlarging to 1.8 instead of the more traditional 2.0. Company car tax categories during the 1980s were based on engine sizes, with three bands – up to 1300cc, up to 1800cc, and over 1801cc, meaning that a top spec Cavalier would cost you less to have than a top spec Sierra, Bluebird or Montego might with its 2.0 lump. And Vauxhall knew how to keep an audience interested with new engines and sporty models. The 1.6SR and plush CD gained 200cc and fuel injection in 1983 to make the SRi and CDi models – 2.0 engines finally became available in 1987, and the SRi gained a boost in late 1987 to become the SRi130. There was even an Irmscher bodykitted variant toward the end of production – the Calibre. Finished in red, low and skirted, the Calibre offered the same sort of kerbside appeal as a Cosworth for a much lower price.

The Calibre was the swansong of a model that had gone further than any other to re-establish Vauxhall as a key player in the fleet car market. The next Cavalier to be launched, the Mk3, was such a step forward that its Opel equivalent got a shiny new name, switching from Ascona to Vectra. Larger than the old model in all directions, much more aerodynamically styled, and much more efficient, GM had waited until the market was used to the look of the Sierra before picking up the baton and running with it. And under the skin were the same engines and a similar drivetrain to that which buyers had by now grown used to under the outgoing model. Surely it could only be onwards and upwards from here?

But that's a story for Family Cars of the 1990s… ■

	Vauxhall Cavalier 1.6	Vauxhall Cavalier 1.8i	Vauxhall Cavalier 2.0i	Vauxhall Cavalier SRi130
CAPACITY	1598cc	1796cc	1996cc	1996cc
POWER	90bhp	115bhp	115bhp	130bhp
TORQUE	99lb.ft	111lb.ft	111lb.ft	133lb.ft
TOP SPEED	106mph	118mph	118mph	117mph

The Peugeot 405 was the car every rep wanted.

Peugeot 405

The prettiest fleet car of the 1980s was also one of the decade's greatest hits.

It sounds trite, but in 1987 the Peugeot 405 really did take our breath away. Here was a family saloon with Pininfarina styling, a chassis tuned by people who knew what they were doing, and a range of willing engines closely linked to those fitted to the all-time hot hatch great, the Peugeot 205GTi. Not only did it look like an Alfa Romeo, but the interior had been created by former BMW and Mercedes impresario Paul Bracq, giving the car even more company car park cred.

To think that of all things, the politics of the motor industry meant that British buyers were meant to view this car as a replacement for the Talbot Solara, a machine that was so beige it's a wonder there wasn't a promotional tie-in with Farah slacks. The Peugeot could scarcely have been different. It was also intended as a replacement for the Peugeot 305; another car with an achingly conservative countenance inside and out but with a much

Even low spec models looked special.

more focused drivetrain than its British progenitor. For such a pair of deliberately rectilinear shapes to have been replaced by something of such striking executive beauty was a shock to the industry. Not, admittedly, an

unwelcome one – but for a family saloon to be this achingly pretty was a novelty that has rarely been repeated since.

And yes, the plastics inside were a bit cheap on the early cars. But this was modern design done

properly and without scaring the client base – a car that looked reassuringly expensive and yet cost buttons to run, so buyers could forgive the odd quality foible if the car was otherwise well assembled. Especially if fitted

with one of the excellent 1.9-litre diesel options – the Peugeot XUD was widely regarded as the best diesel engine available in a passenger car in the 1990s and in the spacious and aerodynamic 405 it found itself a natural home. The only way to make this engaging and practical motor car even better was to give it more luggage space – as a saloon with a high loading lip, the early 405 wasn't quite as practical as it could have been. Not only did a facelift in 1992 bring a lower loading lip, but the strikingly handsome estate was one of the most capacious carryalls of its era, with clever torsion bar suspension enabling a flat load bay with no intrusions from suspension struts.

It was obvious that Peugeot would make a fast version – starting with the 1.9SRi which shared its engine and red striping with the 205GTi. Even its lack of alloy wheels wasn't enough to override the street cred of sharing its drivetrain with the best hot hatch in the business. Later, a 16 valve version of this engine would be used to create the Mi16 for 1988, a car with instant appeal if only for the fact its name sounded like a cross between a spy and an assault rifle. Show us a kid who didn't want his dad to come home in one of these, and we'll show you a kid with no imagination. With 160bhp from an engine closely related to that in the 205 T16 Group B rally car, Autocar would praise the MI16 as a car that could "give a BMW 3-series driver a surprise on a B-road". All it needed to make it into a cut price Cossie alternative was four wheel drive – which the MI16x4 of 1989 would offer. Here was a car with sharp styling, a great interior,

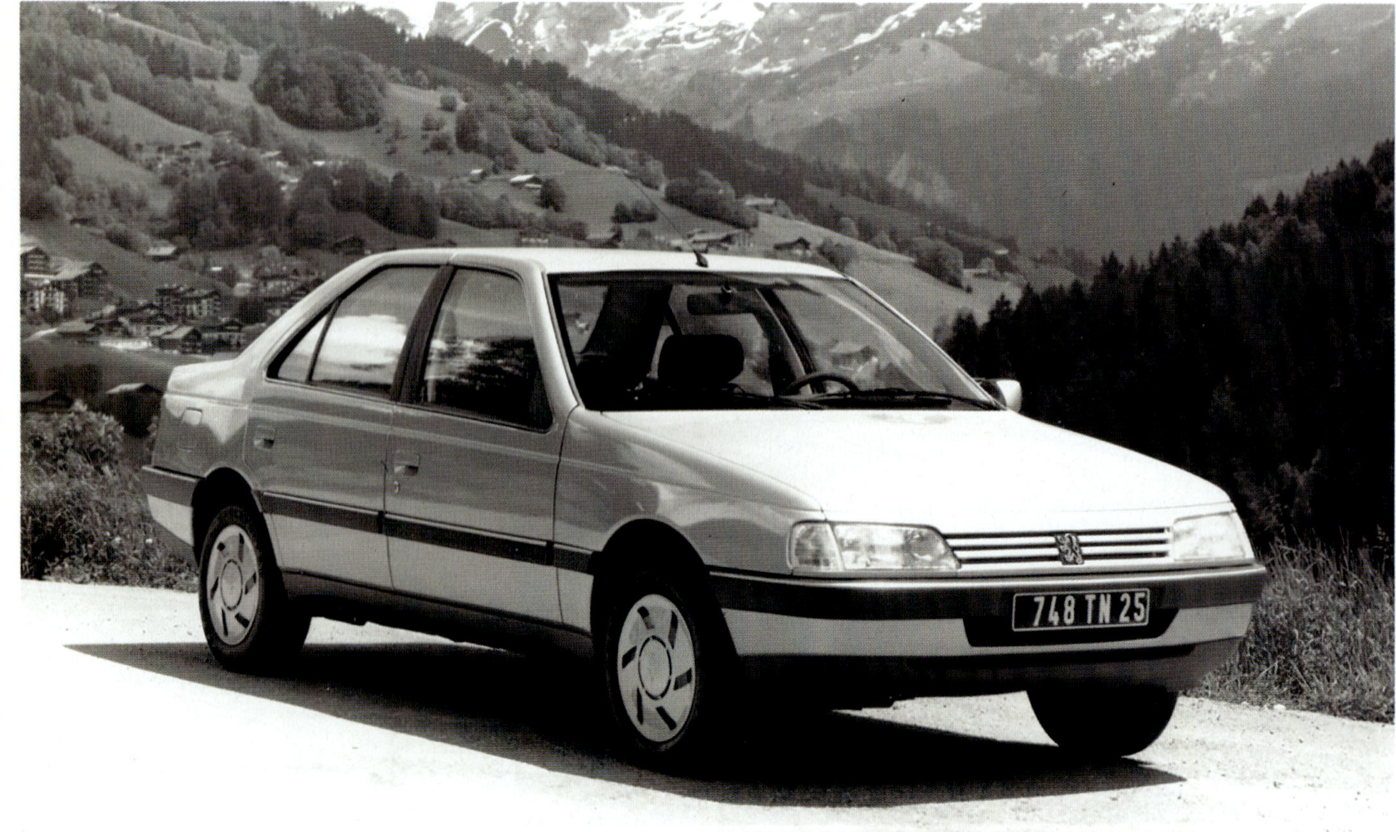

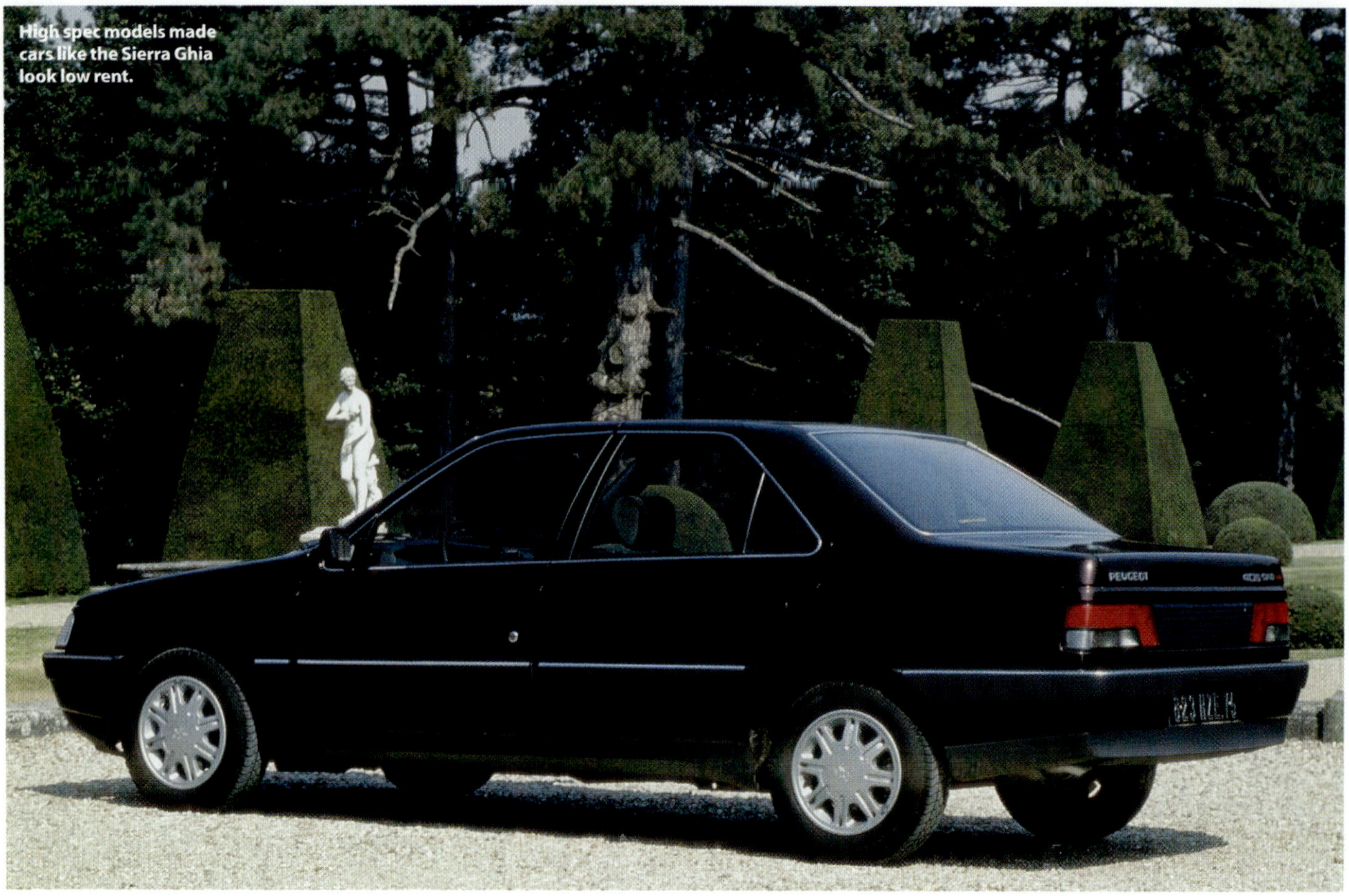
High spec models made cars like the Sierra Ghia look low rent.

unstoppable grip and a fantastic engine – and it was based on a car meant for salesman.

But even that wasn't the best of the bunch, because there was a genuine Cosworth rival for continental 405 fanciers. The 405 T16 was never available in Britain, but it mixed the Mi16x4 formula with a turbocharger, taking output to the same 200bhp as the hot Sierra in a package that was far, far more subtle – no lairy arches or spoilers, just a set of tasteful alloy wheels and headlamp washers to give the game away. Far rarer too, with only 1046 built and none officially heading to the UK. Children dropped off at school in the back of their parents' 1.6GEs or 1.9GRis could dream about a genuinely great halo model – unless your dad was a Peugeot executive and didn't mind left hand drive, you'd simply never get to see one here. We know of just two T16s in the whole of Britain.

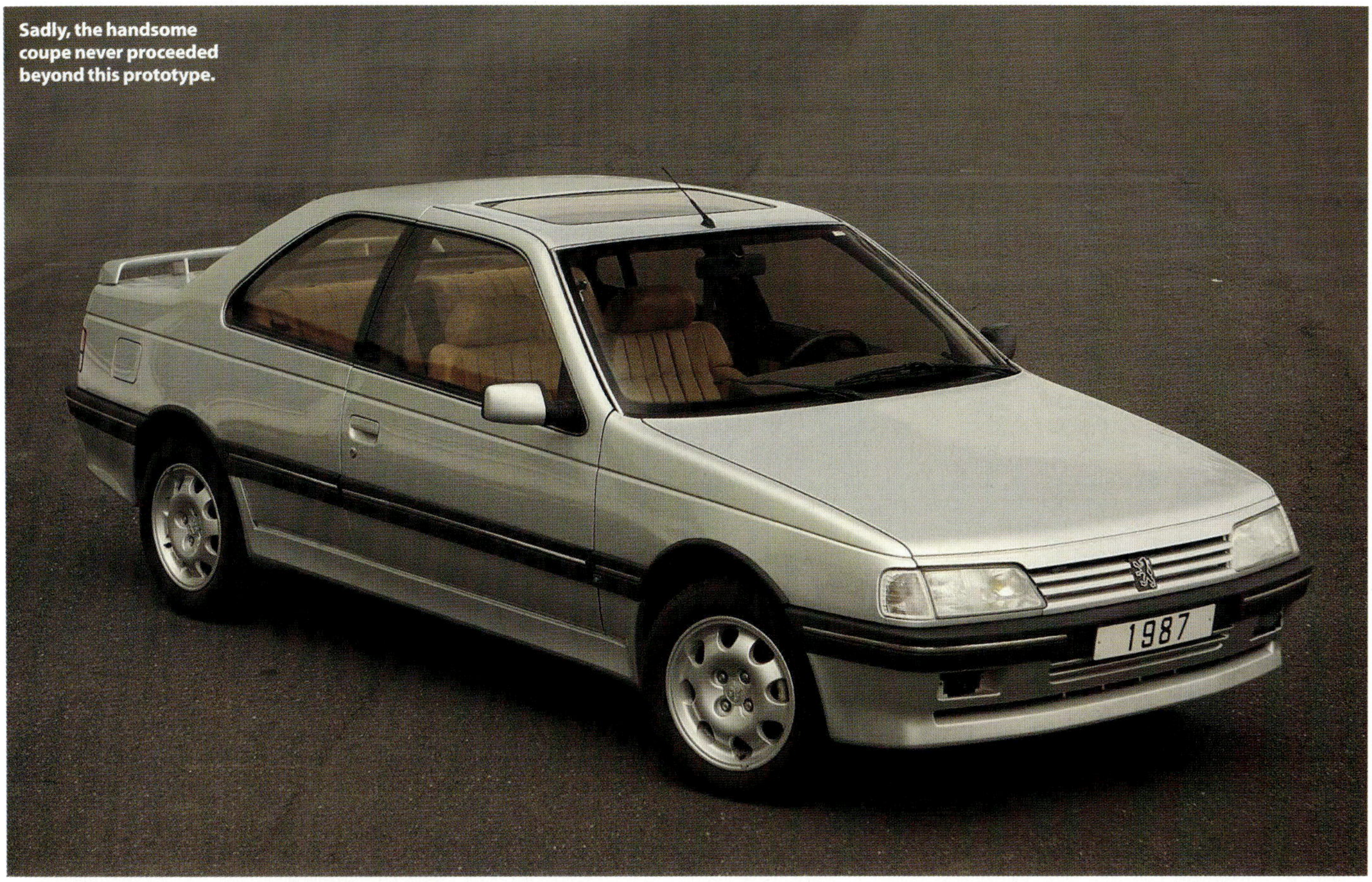

Sadly, the handsome coupe never proceeded beyond this prototype.

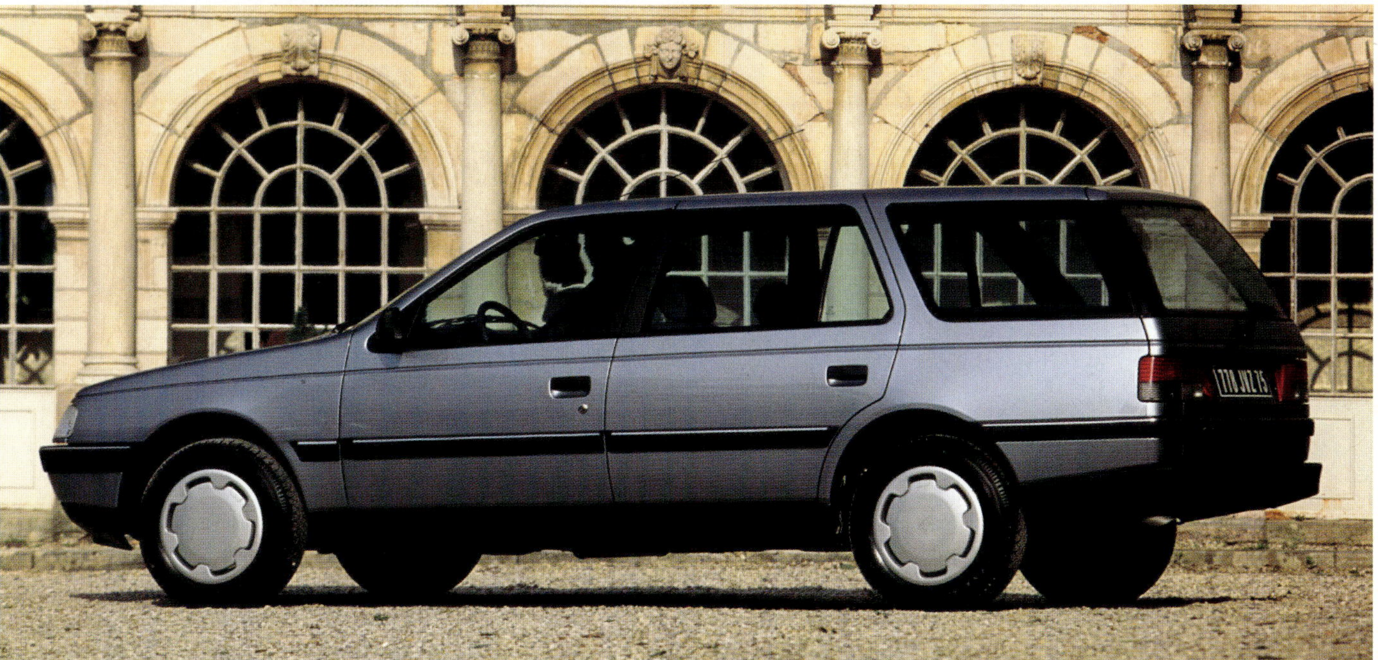

A 405 diesel estate was arguably Europe's greatest taxi.

When it came to replacing the 405 – having outlasted most of its 1980s competitors right into the middle of the 1990s – Peugeot saw little need to mess with the formula that had evidently worked so well. The 406 would offer the same range of saloons and estates, the same great ride, the same stylish looks and the same great value. Meanwhile, it wasn't the end of the Peugeot 405 story – because Iran, Argentina, Egypt and Zimbabwe kept building their own variants into the new Millennium.

Because when you're building a car that could take your breath away, why change a thing? ■

	Peugeot 405 1.4	Peugeot 405 1.6	Peugeot 405 1.9	Peugeot 405 Mi16	Peugeot 405 1.9D	Peugeot 405 1.9TD
CAPACITY	1360cc	1580cc	1905cc	1905cc	1905cc	1905cc
POWER	74bhp	92bhp	125bhp	160bhp	70bhp	92bhp
TORQUE	82lb.ft	99lb.ft	130lb.ft	133lb.ft	88lb.ft	132lb.ft
TOP SPEED	105mph	107mph	118mph	134mph	102mph	109mph

The look of trepidation on the man's face says it all.

talbot alpine and solara

Bland of hope and glory they may have been, but they briefly met a need for British families.

It seems odd that while the Chrysler Alpine had arguably been ahead of its time, by the time the competition caught up the Alpine no longer looked like an appealing prospect. Front wheel drive large family hatchbacks were not what the average British motorist had wanted on its launch in 1976, favouring the staid conservatism of the Ford Cortina and the Vauxhall Cavalier. And as if the concept of a big hatch hadn't been bad enough, Chrysler had wanted to inflict a car with white plastic bumpers on a buying public still defiantly used to the chrome it had always known. Buyers knew the car had fundamentally been designed by the French and rebelled against the idea of something they felt unsuited to the British market – it simply wasn't going to work for them.

Two years later, Chrysler came to a similar conclusion and divested its European arm entirely, retreating back across the Atlantic and leaving Peugeot holding the baby. In 1979 Peugeot would rebrand all existing models from the new

Solara's three box shape offered variety, at least...

Alpine through to the ageing Hunter as Talbots – by which point in time the Alpine had already lost its forward-raked nose and up to the minute plastic bumpers in favour of something derivative and staid. A new grille, new lights and new bumpers made the car look much more conventional – and while it bore

the same vague air of depression as the Austin Ambassador it was at least less divisive than what had come before. For 1980 there would also be a saloon variant – the Solara would finally replace the Hillman Hunter with a plain three box reworking of the Alpine that resembled a Tagora in miniature – Talbot bosses

forgetting that the Tagora was about as desirable as a dose of leprosy with the British public.

It's not entirely clear how Talbot expected to get away with marketing a depressingly conformist saloon variant of an already unpopular yet more practical hatchback as a premium choice, but it tried to do so

TALBOT ALPINE

By the 1980s a vinyl roof was decidedly passé, but Talbot tried.

anyway – marketing the Solara at a higher price than the equivalent Alpine model by model in a bid to render the new model utterly pointless. But by the 1980s, just as the rest of the world was switching on to the family hatchback, the Alpine's popularity fell even further. Now an old design with what was seen as a coarse engine and with factory closures affecting public trust in

the company, it was to be the last Talbot production car as well as the first of the revived era.

You don't even need to consider the school playground or the company car park to understand that ownership of a Talbot of any type was seen as social suicide in the United Kingdom. The Alpine and Solara in particular had earned a reputation as the transport of

the uncaring – cars for people to whom terms such as style, power and elegance held simply no meaning in an automotive context. And on the basis that underneath it all, the Alpine and Solara were not actually bad cars for people seeking nothing more than a means of getting from A to B, it wasn't necessarily unfair to bestow such a noncommittal image upon them. To claim

you were a car enthusiast and to drive a Solara was akin to claiming you were passionate about Italian food as you tucked into a pizza margherita.

In desperation in 1985, Talbot looked to its past in a bid to inject a little style into the model. Remembering its 1950s mid liners, the Hillman Minx and Sunbeam Rapier, it felt that rebranding the new cars

By the end just two models were available - the entry level Minx pictured here and the range-topping Rapier.

with names it was using thirty years earlier was clearly the way to attract a new and youthful kind of buyer. The Minx had wheel trims and – often – beige paintwork, while the Rapiers got nicer velour seats, alloys, and metallic paint in a number of two-tone choices. It was however too little, too late – it looked like the cheap tart-up job it really was, and the young, energetic buyers Talbot was hoping it could court simply bought cars like the Vauxhall Cavalier instead.

	Talbot Alpine 1.3	Talbot Solara 1.6
CAPACITY	1294cc	1592cc
POWER	68bhp	87bhp
TORQUE	79lb.ft	101lb.ft
TOP SPEED	93mph	98mph

Entirely unsurprisingly, when it came to replacing the Talbot models barely a year after the final range changes were made, Peugeot simply didn't bother. Not only that, but it took active steps to rid the world of Talbot cars in their entirely. People wanting a hatchback or something unusual were steered into the unconventionally suspended Citroën BX, while those looking for conventionality were encouraged to buy the similarly severely styled Peugeot 305 in saloon or estate guises instead. Talbot had been

preparing a replacement for its smaller Horizon; the Arizona was hastily rebranded as the Peugeot 309 and offered as a curious halfway house between the larger 305 and the smaller 205 with which it shared its doors. The small Samba was canned, with buyers instead being nudged toward the Peugeot 205. For the last six years of the marque's existence, there would only be one model – the Express, a rebadged Citroën C25 van most fondly remembered now as the basis for scores of camper vans and motorhomes. ■

austin maestro and montego

A revolution for the former British Leyland: The Maestro and Montego were resolutely conservative.

Even the most ardent British Leyland admirer would admit that its middle line range was in something of a mess during the 1970s. There was the forward thinking Austin Allegro, which competed almost perfectly with the Morris Marina – underpinned with the post war componentry of the Morris Minor and the out of date engines from the MG sports cars. If neither of these appealed, there was the Maxi – marketed as a lifestyle choice, its primary purpose was to justify BL offering no other hatchbacks. And then there was the Princess, which didn't know if it was meant to compete with the Cortina or the Granada. That's before we get on to the Triumph Toledo and Dolomite models, busily trying to steal sales from within. Because of the range complexity BL's profit margins were… difficult… not helped by

the fact that the fleet managers of Britain liked the simplicity offered by Ford and Vauxhall. What BL needed was a sensible and rational replacement for its four mid range Austin Morris products, and it got it.

By fundamentally copying the underpinnings of the Golf and matching them to modernised versions of the Allegro's engines, it was able to launch the Maestro in 1983. And despite its swish plastic bumpers, nice metallic paint and optional digital talking

Injected 2.0 MGs were quicker than the Golf GTi.

There were extension panels to bridge the gap between the slam panel and the headlamps, and a solid foot of storage space between the spare wheel and the back of the area under the boot floor. The styling by committee approach – courtesy of David Bache, Ian Beech and Roy Axe – was formal and stately at best, but nobody could really call it beautiful with its pseudo wrap-round rear window and its plastic windowsills to disguise the origin of the Maestro doors. Its new one piece dashboard was a vast improvement over the original, with generally better layout and far fewer trim rattles, and would make its way into the Maestro too by 1986.

Top of the three for both Maestro and Montego came

dash (Standard on the range-topping Vanden Plas and MG), it was simplicity on wheels.

While the Maestro was perfect as a competitor to the Escort, Astra and Golf, it wouldn't do as a replacement for the Ital or the Ambassador – desperate interim facelifts for the Marina and Princess. The Montego had to be bigger – and to draw a distinction, Austin Rover decided it would be a saloon. Much of the substructure was identical, though the wheelbase was slightly lengthened and the new panelwork was much longer than the substructure really needed.

Limited run Turbo was an instant classic.

Two tone paint helped to disguise Montego's origins.

the MG variants – at launch, the MG Maestro 1600 and MG Montego Efi. Both had alloy wheels, front and rear spoilers, red carpets, red seatbelts, and sports seats. Both initially also had digital dashboard, though the Montego would lose its much more advanced example after just 9 months. It made up for this in 1985 though with the launch of the new MG Montego Turbo – 152bhp, the same as a V8 SD1 but from just 2.0, and all driven through the front wheels. If it sounds wayward, it was – but it was the fastest four door MG saloon for very nearly the next twenty years. The same year, the Maestro got the 2.0Efi engine from the MG Montego to replace the carburetted 1.6 in the early cars. 1989 saw the real high water mark for performance – a limited edition run of MG Maestros fitted with the turbocharged engine from the Montego, a big Tickford-styled bodykit, and mean 15" cross spoke alloys. Just 505 of these ripsnorting road burners were built and even when the

A lazy facelift and the loss of Austin badging fooled nobody.

average Maestro was one of the cheapest bangers in the back of AutoTrader, a Maestro Turbo was a collectible classic.

The standard cars, though, had an image problem. Despite having a capable chassis and plenty of space, the Maestro and Montego were tarnished by the reputation left behind by their predecessors and the occasional minor glitch in quality didn't help either. Top spec Vanden Plas models were seen as jokes – despite offering more walnut and leather than any other car in their class and lashings of chrome, they were about as desirable as a bus pass. An attempt in 1987 to drop the Austin badging from the cars and a further attempt in 1988 to pull them into the Rover family with one of the laziest facelifts ever applied to a car both read as what they were; desperate attempts to make the idea of Maestro or Montego ownership palatable in a world where the word Austin summoned up images of rotting Allegros. Unwilling to sully the Rover brand in public the two models were sold as unbadged orphans, while the new Rover 200 and 400 models soaked up the image conscious buyers on their behalf. Rover replaced both Maestro and Montego – with the Rover 200 and Rover 600 – yet it kept the original models on sale as budget alternatives appealing to a smaller and smaller audience well into the 1990s.

It was easy to mock – especially as in Britain self deprecation has become something of a national sport – and yet underneath the image problem there was noting wrong with either car. The Maestro and Montego drove well, with predictable handling and a soft ride, plenty of space and low maintenance bills. Sensible and rational – and doomed from the start by the sins of the fathers. ■

	Maestro 1.3	Maestro 1.6	Montego 2.0	Montego 2.0i	Montego diesel	Maestro Turbo
CAPACITY	1275cc	1598cc	1994cc	1994cc	1994cc	1994cc
POWER	69bhp	86bhp	104bhp	113bhp	81bhp	152bhp
TORQUE	75lb.ft	91lb.ft	121lb.ft	134lb.ft	116lb.ft	169lb.ft
TOP SPEED	96mph	105mph	108mph	112mph	102mph	131mph

renault espace

Above all others, this family car represented an instant shift in family car thinking.

As we will explain in the appropriate chapter, it was hard for British businessmen to justify buying the larger Renault 25 in the British marketplace. It was equally difficult to justify buying a Renault 21. After all, if you wanted a French car that handled well you bought yourself a Peugeot 405. If you wanted a French car that rode superbly, you bought a Citroën BX. And if you didn't want a French car, you bought something like the Vauxhall Cavalier. And nobody bought a Renault 11 over an Escort or a Golf in Britain. There was nothing objectively wrong with any of them, they were just cars you considered before buying something else. If your dad was a Renault dealer in the 1980s, bonus cheques were rare occasions.

There was one family friendly car, however, that Renault dealers really didn't have to fight to sell. Not only was it an excellent concept, but one that the rest of the world simply hadn't seen coming. Not except for a Brit called Fergus Pollock, who had created the concept while working for

Rootes-Chrysler in the 1970s and not except for Matra, which had originally developed Pollock's concept for Chrysler as a replacement for the Matra Rancho. But then PSA bought Chrysler Europe and promptly rebranded all its products as Talbots. Looking at the risky, daring new monobox concept, PSA said "no thanks", and Renault said "yes please", swiftly adapting mechanical componentry from the Renault 18 saloon and Fuego coupe. The new car that got the markets talking was the Espace.

On the face of it, a single box vehicle that was the size of a van felt like an unusual competitor for the family estate car. And with prices starting at £10,145 – similar to a Sierra Ghia estate or a BMW 320i – it was a high price to pay for a car that many buyers didn't entirely understand at first. But then people started to pay attention to it; to see that while a Montego Vanden Plas EFi estate offered seven seats for the same sort of money, it couldn't offer the same sort of versatility. Because here was a car that could not only seat seven, but

Clever duotone paint schemes helped to hide its van-like shape.

in which the seats could swivel to allow families to huddle together facing each other on picnics in the rain. In which the seats could fold down to make a bed for a forward-planning couple on holiday. And in which, if you left all the back seats in the garage, you could moonlight at weekends as a man with a van. It might not have looked especially sexy – there's only so much you can do with a monobox shape – but it offered options that no other car would match.

It allowed kids to brag in a very different way, too. While there might have been a child in the playground whose dad had a V8 Rover and took them up the M1 in it at stupid speeds, Espace families would spend their weekends kayaking, or on cycle trails, or doing anything else that could be done with the space an Espace could offer. And better still, because it was a seven seater, they could take their friends with them. The Espace would fit in the garage, too – at just once inch longer than a Vauxhall Belmont but ten inches higher, it was easier to park than even a standard Sierra while offering acres more interior room. And the Douvrin engines fitted to all petrol Espaces were simple, reliable units, not perhaps the last word in power or refinement but certainly up to the standard of the era. You could even have all wheel drive in the Espace Quadra of 1987.

And better still, the plastic body panels didn't rot. Unfortunately,

Space for seven, and even some suitcases.

Espace could be had - in rare cases - with all-wheel drive. Few Espace Quadras survive today.

Games room, office, bed, the Espace had your needs covered.

Facelift helped to lose the Chrysler look at the nose.

the steel underpinnings did. But that's not why there are very few Espaces left today. It's something different. Take a look at any proper family car – anything that was only ever really designed for family use. We're not talking about repmobiles, or cars owned by pensioners, these are the cars that end up sitting in garages and emerging twenty years later in perfect condition. Cars targeted at families get sold on to poorer families, they get used and used and used until they breathe their last and go to scrap. You never see an Espace because they were so good at their job, they were never allowed to retire.

Look forward into the 1990s and 2000s. Look at the number of imitators the Espace spawned from every corner of the globe. Not only were there scores of MPVs, but the versatility was extended to smaller cars including Renault's own Scenic. It could be argued that no car had quite such a significant impact on the immediate development of family motoring as the Renault Espace, and while today the market focus has shifted to far cooler SUVs, the majority lack the innovative uses of interior space that were pioneered by the Renault Espace and continued by the cars it directly inspired. The Espace itself would continue through several generations before being withdrawn in the UK in 2012 at the end of fourth generation production. In left hand drive countries, the sixth generation Espace is still a strong seller today. ∎

	Renault Espace
CAPACITY	1995cc
POWER	110bhp
TORQUE	120lb.ft
TOP SPEED	113mph

Maestro van headlamps and 110 top windows hid Range Rover underpinings.

slower sellers – fleet favourites

We don't have space to give every family classic its own section in this title. Here are some of the best of the rest in the fleet sector.

The 1980s were an interesting time for family car design, and while the Ford Sierra had shown that being radical wasn't always the way forward in a very conservative sector of the market there were some manufacturers who tried to do something just a little bit different in order to attract buyers.

Land Rover had a trick up its sleeve as well, right at the end of the decade. We will look in the next section at how the Range Rover – particularly in Vogue SE form – redefined the concept of the family luxury car. But Land Rover realised it could extend this concept downwards. The Discovery of 1989 owed a lot to its big brother under the ski, with V8 and diesel engines plus the chassis by and large

The stripes were an acquired taste...

NISSAN PRAIRIE

The car that almost invented the mini MPV.

borrowed from big brother. Yes it was a three door model and yes it had an unusual stepped roof arrangement – and yes, there was a blue interior that stretched the limits of what could be called taste even further than the dodgy graphics on the side. But for top end Sierra money here was a car that offered the same Lrod of the Manor experience as the Range Rover, in a much more middle class manner. It was a car that attracted a waiting list, too, meaning that if you could get the company car fleet manager to stump up for one, he'd probably let you have it for the sake of the residuals. Here was a family car that took an existing recipe and made It much more accessible.

Unlike the Nissan Prairie – probably the biggest own goal of the decade. On the face of it there was much to commend it for – a compact yet tall MPV style body, with no B-pillars, making access a doddle even for the elderly and infirm and made accessing child seat latches and fastenings a piece of cake. It looked inoffensive if Japanese, and with its 1.8 litre engine it went well enough for what it was. Where the British importer messed up was in reading the market. Seven seat variants were available in Japan, and would

have put a sizeable dent in the sales of the larger and more expensive Renault Espace. Bear in mind that in 1985, an entry level Espace GTS was £10145 while the very priciest Prairie Anniversary could be had for £8499 – the price of a Montego 1.6HL estate. But when it came

to selecting the models and trims for import, the British concession decided it would be best to market the Prairie as a five seat estate with a big boot, thus nullifying any real reason for people to buy it over a Bluebird. As such, what could have been the cleverest family

car of the 1980s was relegated to the backwaters, its biggest market being the wheelchair conversion industry. It would take until the Vauxhall Zafira of 1999 for buyers to be offered a tall, compact MPV with the option of seven seats. The Prairie deserved much, much more… ∎

Unsurprisingly, Prairies were popular with wheelchair users.

In Vogue special editions were the first to use the name.

range rover

Intended for farmers and evolved into the city, the Range Rover arguably did more to shift attitudes toward family cars than any other model.

There is one car above all the others in this title that predicted the shape of family cars to come – one car that heralded a change a quarter of a century ahead of time, an aspirational machine that ultimately would herald the end of the family saloon. And while the sport utility vehicles it ultimately inspired are far worse in every way than the hatchbacks and saloons they replaced, the Range Rover arguably became one of the era's defining luxury family cars.

Because let's look at it compared to the alternatives. By 1988 a Vogue SE cost £28855, the same sort of money as a Jaguar Sovereign or a Maserati 425. And with 14mpg thirst on the best of days, eight cylinders to service and lots of expensive toys that can break, it should be considered in the same sort of vein as these large, expensive saloon cars rather than as a simple and honest son of the soil. Only one of those cars has space in the back for man's best friend as well as the suitcases. Only one can handle a double buggy for the kids when they're young.

Brochures emphasised the car's go-anywhere nature.

Only one can cope with a tip run. While it was the most expensive family car to warrant its own feature in this title, it was and remains to this day one of the most versatile too.

The Range Rover originated in 1970 as a car that offered the best of both worlds to farmers – saving them from having to buy a car as well as the Land Rover. Unsurprisingly the concept took off, with plenty of aftermarket companies offering such things as four door conversions, plush trim and even convertibles adorned with Ford Granada front ends.

But it was the marketing men at Land Rover in the 1980s that really shaped the car and helped it to find its niche. After all, why shouldn't Land Rover have a slice of the lucrative pie being carved up by the converters? By giving it four doors and plush seats, carpets and wood

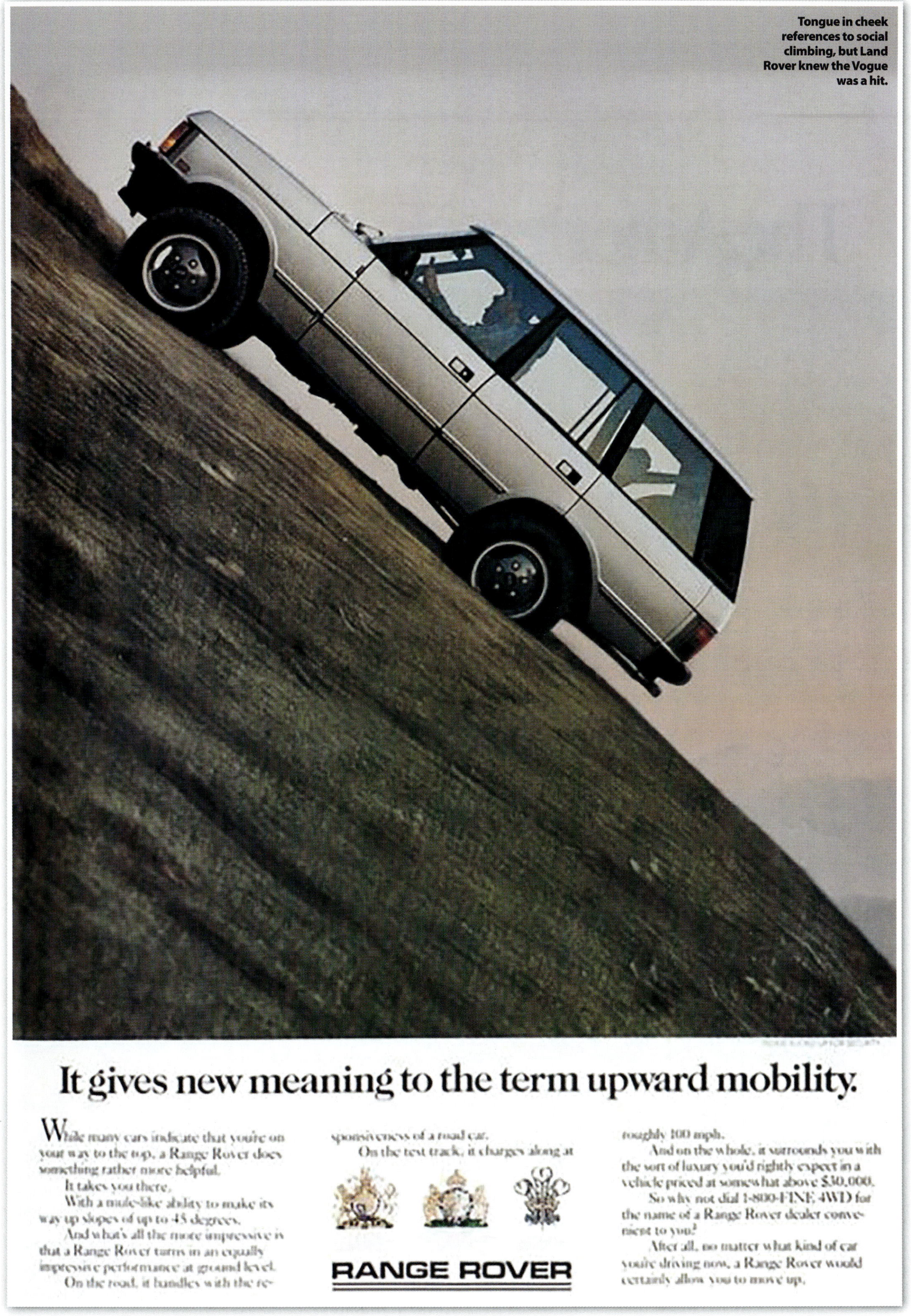

It gives new meaning to the term upward mobility.

While many cars indicate that you're on your way to the top, a Range Rover does something rather more helpful.

It takes you there.

With a mule-like ability to make its way up slopes of up to 45 degrees.

And what's all the more impressive is that a Range Rover turns in an equally impressive performance at ground level.

On the road, it handles with the responsiveness of a road car.

On the test track, it charges along at roughly 100 mph.

And on the whole, it surrounds you with the sort of luxury you'd rightly expect in a vehicle priced at somewhat above $30,000.

So why not dial 1-800-FINE-4WD for the name of a Range Rover dealer convenient to you?

After all, no matter what kind of car you're driving now, a Range Rover would certainly allow you to move up.

RANGE ROVER

Last models were given a bigger engine, air suspension and a longer wheelbase - the Vogue LSE.

as factory options, it shifted the car into the ideal transport for the *gentleman* farmer, or the city boy with a pad in the countryside harbouring desires of gentrydom. Yes, it could still climb Snowdon, but now it could slink through Soho the following day without seeming out of place. The plush velour seats, automatic gearbox and colour coded wheels gave it street cred to match its field cred, and they soon became as common a sight in SW3 as in the Shires.

By the time they reached their second or third owners, their loadbays had often been compromised by the fitment of LPG tanks to try to halve the fuel bills; drinking like Oliver Reed is acceptable if you're on the Sunday Times rich list but if you were the sort of person who might be buying a secondhand Range Rover the odds were you couldn't afford the bills attracted by a new one. Over time, they became less and less cared for, and more and more tired, and many Range Rover Classics have since been scrapped. But the survivors are now changing hands for silly money, warranting restorations that would have seemed insane even a decade ago.

The first upmarket Range Rover was the In Vogue limited edition of 1981, but it was the "production" Vogue and later Vogue SE model that earned the Range Rover its place in the car park at Benenden and on the sidelines at Ascot. Their V8 engines and all wheel drive drivetrains meant that they weren't cheap cars to run – with 20mpg on a good day the best

Extended wheelbase hid what was essentially a testbed for the second generation cars.

Unlike with a prestige saloon, it's hard to be snowed in with a Range Rover.

Walnut and leather marked the Range Rover Vogue out from its rivals.

you could realistically expect – but they really did offer the buying public a new kind of family car experience. As the 1980s gave way to the 1990s the car became more and more upmarket, and by the time of the second generation car of 1994 the pretence had gone – this was now a luxury car that could handle the odd off roading session, rather than a utilitarian tool that had been sexed up. The P38a would build upon the themes tentatively explored with the long wheelbase Range Rover LSE – with air suspension, bigger engines and more toys, it was actively targeted at buyers of S-class Mercs and Jaguar XJs.

And the touch paper had been lit on the off road revolution. Land Rover itself capitalised on the car's desirability as an on-road companion with the cheaper Discovery of 1989 which we mentioned in the previous section; with its Conran designed blue interior, its stripes and its Alpine roof it turned Range Rover underpinnings into a middle class staple. It wasn't just Land Rover; everybody from Ford (Explorer) to Mercedes-Benz (ML-class) would develop a family friendly 4x4 of their own in the 1990s, and after the millennium conventional saloons would give way in more and more cases to the practicality afforded by what was fundamentally a tall and high riding estate car. Eventually the craze would extend downwards, with even the best-selling Ford Fiesta usurped by the pseudo off road Ecosport. And it was this car, the Range Rover, that set that ball rolling. Not only was it the best 4x4xFar, but the car that directly shaped how we see family transport to this day. ■

	Range Rover 3.5	Range Rover 3.9i
CAPACITY	3528cc	3948cc
POWER	165bhp	185bhp
TORQUE	207lb.ft	235lb.ft
TOP SPEED	106mph	110mph

bmw e30

The red brace hero that made your dad king of the playground.

If Gordon Gekko had traded in the Square Mile then the cars would have been smaller, the currency arguably stronger, the lady much more Iron, but the braces would have been just as red. The common concept of the young urban professional – the yuppie – stood just as strongly in London as it did in New York, and the car park of Fundamental and Marshall held more BMW 3-series as a result than the factory car park in Munich.

Greed, for lack of a better word, was good – and wearing your wallet on your sleeve was a key element of life for the 1980s stockbroker, city trader or financier. This era of conspicuous consumption tied in nicely with a shift in the market – prices for imported cars were coming down in the EEC era, and companies such as BMW, Audi and Mercedes were offering smaller models that were more affordable than such marques had traditionally been. No longer was it necessary for people who

had reached a certain point in their carers to leave behind the Sierra in favour of the Ford Granada or the Vauxhall Carlton; it was possible to buy a car that looked like a genuine step up for

the same sort of money. And if a Granada showed the neighbours you were doing well in life, just imagine how the net curtains of Surrey would glow red with the envy of the neighbours admiring

your brand new BMW. It's no surprise that company car user choosers chose to use an E30.

And there was an impressive range from which to choose. Most conventional and most

Roof down or up, the factory convertible looked good.

Twin headlamps were standard, in a departure from the previous E21 model.

popular were the saloon models, available in sporting two-door and sensible four-door guise, with chrome window frames for the classy and blacked out "Shadowline" frames for the stealthy. Thosewho needed a modicum more space went for the Touring; a lifestyle estate that made up for its inability to swallow a wardrobe by looking incredibly cool. Initially, open 3-series motoring came in the form of the Baur Cabriolet, with fixed rear wide windows and a Triumph Stag style roll over frame. From 1985 the factory introduced its own convertible, which featured a full folding roof.

So what if the E30 was smaller than the Sierra that such traders had traded up from? So what if it looked less substantial in the corporate car park than a Carlton? In terms of image, that kidney grille was cast iron – in the same way that a bottle of Taittinger will always look better than a full case of plonk from the nearest Oddbins ever could. A BMW 316 cost the same sort of money as a Granada 2.0L, and while it was a smaller car with far lower equipment levels, the badge spoke clearly of your standing. And to give an idea of just how high BMW had set its small car's bar – the range-topping 325i SE was £300 more than an XJ6 2.9, and looked little

different to the 316 you could have bought for Ford money. And if you really needed to justify to yourself why you were driving the entry level Bimmer, you could always ask whether a smaller car didn't actually make more sense with Central London parking.

And while BMW was not alone – you could equally have bought an Audi 80 or a Mercedes-Benz 190 – it was the BMW that captured the imagination of the upwardly mobile better than the

others. Here was a car capable of carrying the family, a car that could be had for the same money as your dad's Granada, with the same sort of premium image as imports costing almost twice as much. After all, Audis were still just a little bit worthy and well-meaning despite the best efforts of the Quattro, and a Mercedes saloon was about as "old man" as a cardigan despite the fact that it was the newest kid on the block. While

Early open E30s were converted by Baur and retained side windows.

the City boys used their 325is as a stepping stone toward the Porsche 924 (Or, for the brand loyal red bracer, an M3), those driving models at the lower end of the range saw them as well-made, practical cars that – with a personal plate – would continue to keep them at the top of the social ladder on The Avenue for years to come.

Not that time would continue to treat these cars so kindly. They were clear targets for thieves, and as the 1980s moved into the 1990s the basic 316s and 318s became the sort of cars that teenage wideboys would adorn with fat exhausts and silly Max Power wheels. They thought that having a BMW would help their street cred too, but the truth was that their ownership only dented the image of the brand. It was this, and a shift toward mass marketing tactics and easy finance, that led to BMW's slip from the top of the prestige hierarchy. Just a decade after the last E30s were built, BMW found itself grubbing for corporate sales against the Mondeo and the Vectra, with the 318i the most popular model on a now devalued platform. The inevitability of such a slide is obvious in any country obsessed with social image, but the E30 itself stands strong as the high watermark for BMW's smallest saloon. ■

	BMW 316	BMW 318i	BMW 320i	BMW 325i	BMW M3
CAPACITY	1766cc	1766cc	1990cc	2494cc	2302cc
POWER	90bhp	101bhp	125bhp	171bhp	200bhp
TORQUE	82lb.ft	103lb.ft	123lb.ft	164lb.ft	177lb.ft
TOP SPEED	103mph	111mph	121mph	132mph	140mph

Saloons like this late model Scorpio were much more palatable to executive tastes.

ford granada mk3

Bigger than the Sierra… but was it seen as quite such a serious mis-step?

It's fair to say that in the early 1980s there existed an air of trepidation within Ford of Europe. The Sierra had launched in 1982 to general bewilderment, and while the market was thawing toward it through good fleet deals, the fact remained that Ford had to introduce the ultra-conservative Orion in order to stem the tide of buyers lost to the competition. And the Sierra figured more strongly in Ford's future plans than it wanted to admit – the replacement for its range-topping Granada saloon and estate would be another aerodynamic hatchback spun from a larger version of the Sierra floorpan.

The new car was to be called the Scorpio, but in desperation British product planners sought to retain the Granada name instead – hoping that keeping the old name would instil a sense of brand loyalty in its customer base, who would feel reassured by the badge that this

What we knew as the Granada was marketed overseas as the Scorpio in all trim levels.

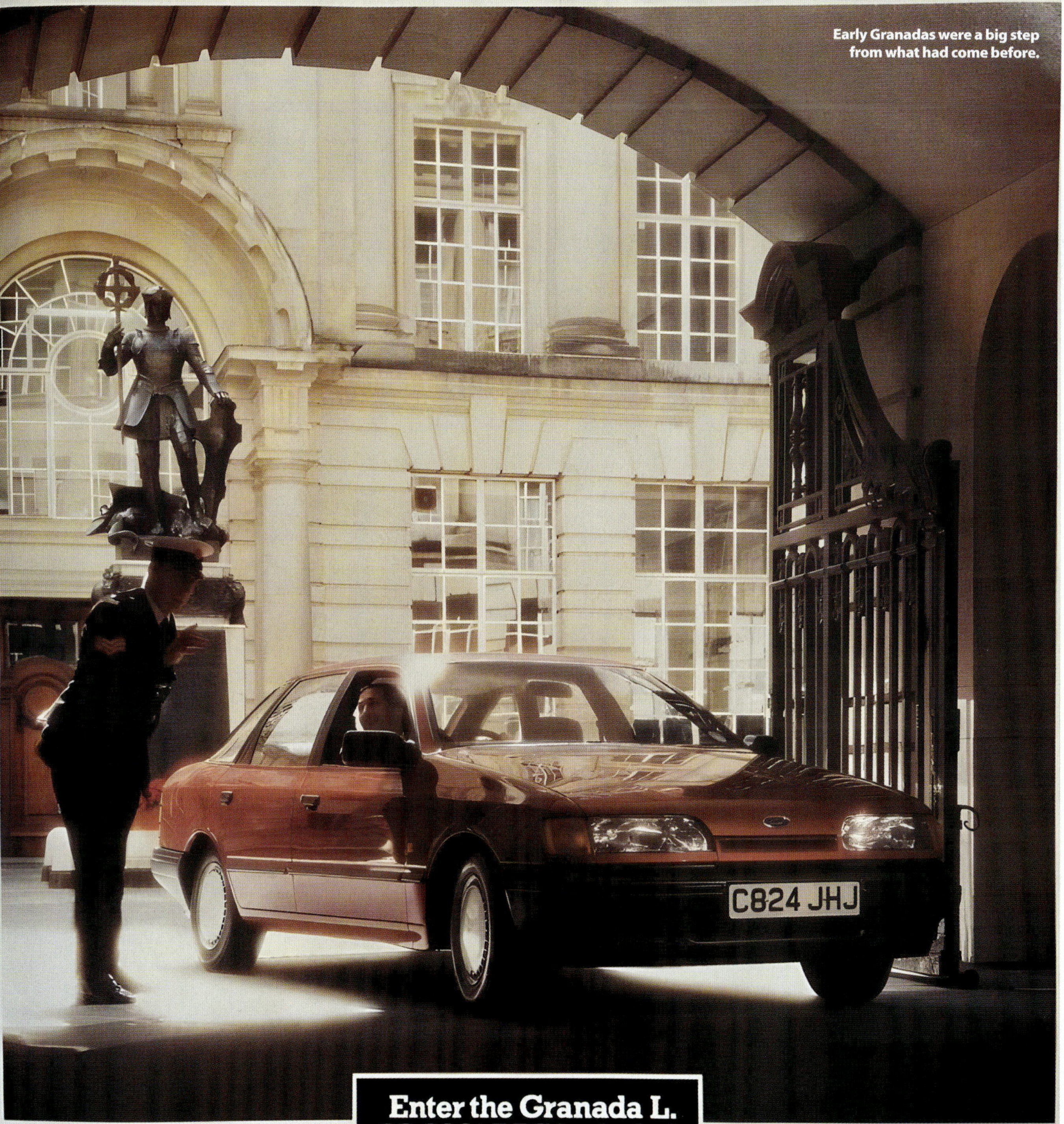

Early Granadas were a big step from what had come before.

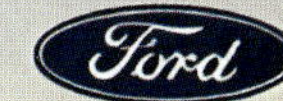

Enter the Granada L. £8,899,* ABS included.

The new Granada L boasts all the essential qualities that make a Granada a Granada. And for which it was voted 'Car of the Year, 1986', one of more than a dozen awards.

The anti-lock brakes are just one example of the car's sophistication. They're the ones that could help you steer out of trouble if you have to swerve while making a panic stop.

You get the same smooth, big car ride from the same supple suspension you find in every Granada. There's the same quietness from the flush fitting glass, and the same generous leg-room – quite exceptional in the back.

And, of course, there are all those thoughtful little Ford touches that count so much – the low friction seat belts that don't tug at your shoulder, the steering column that adjusts for height as well as reach and the Chubb high-security locking system, to name but three.

For your £8,899* you also get the 1.8 litre lean burn engine which gives you a maximum speed of 111 mph.† And, perhaps more importantly, develops 90% of its maximum torque at only 1800 rpm, so even at low speeds it pulls smoothly in fifth gear – the mark of a refined car.

For a little more money, there's also a 2.0 litre L which has rather more power.

If you'd like to know more see your Ford dealer now. He'll be happy to help you into a Granada.

*Max. retail price, correct at time of going to press, excl. delivery and number plates. †Ford computed figs.

FORD GRANADA. CAR OF THE YEAR 1986. Ford

car really was just a continuation of the ultra conservative Granada saloon under its space age skin. A halfway house compromise was reached, reintroducing the two name tactic from the Mk1 Granada era by marketing all barring the top model as the Granada, and retaining Scorpio as a trim level for the plushest model of all.

And if the Sierra had been controversial, the new Granada was even more so. Even more swish to look at, with a wrap-around glasshouse, flush-fitting windows, and a shape that owed more to the new American Ford Taurus than to Granadas of old. There were three models at launch – GL and Ghia came with different wheel trims and velour trim, and a leather-lined Granada Scorpio at the top of the pile with alloys and thicker chrome trims to the bumpers. The Granada Scorpio name would be retired within the first year though, swapped for the simpler Scorpio moniker and with badging reverse to make Scorpio the prominent name. Entry level L models and V6 4x4s would be introduced at the same time.

Inside, things were rather more normal with large, squashy armchairs, a fairly conventional dashboard and – courtesy of the Sierra – underpinnings that were unrelentingly traditional. It felt like an utterly conventional big car – and if the aerodynamically quiet windows caused consternation, at least there was precedent in the executive class from Audi and its 100. Granadas used a range of four cylinder and V6 petrol engines inherited from the outgoing car, plus a 2.5 litre diesel unit of Peugeot origin – all driving the rear wheels through conventional manual and automatic gearboxes.

The new hatchback body might not have looked quite so formal as what came before, but Ford's marketing men were able to point to cars like the Rover SD1 and

Unsurprisingly, a big, powerful, simple car was popular with the police.

Renault 30 to demonstrate the benefits of the new shape. Who needed a cumbersome estate when the "saloon" equivalent could carry almost anything? And not only was it good for families with space for an adult between two child seats and loads of room for prams in the boot, it was a boon to the private hire trade. The cabbies even had their own 'Taxi' derivative, with a larger centre console with space for a meter and a generally reduced specification to keep the price down. In diesel form, a Granada taxi was pretty much unbeatable for airport runs, with room in the back for the longest of legs and seats comfortable enough to catch forty winks on the way to your 3am flight.

The American look of the Granada and Scorpio was deliberate – because Ford had plans for its new European range topper. It had seen how luxurious European saloons from the likes of Audi and Mercedes-Benz were eclipsing the home grown competition in the premium marketplace, and thought that bringing over its own Euro saloon might help to stem the tide. Selling through Mercury dealerships and using a German derivative of the brand name, the Merkur Scorpio was offered from 1987 to 1989 Stateside. Ford had paved the way for the new car from 1985, offering a much-modified Sierra XR4 as the Merkur XR4Ti – albeit one that had shed its

2.8-litre Cologne V6 for a 2.3 turbocharged Pinto. Sales were modest but consistent, and the project was only halted by forthcoming US safety legislation that would have meant a costly redesign.

Back home in Europe, the Granada range was bolstered in 1989 by the launch of the four door saloon – conservatively styled and with a small vestigial grille in the manner of the Sierra Sapphire, it went some way to bringing back the traditional buyers who had fled Ford for the new three box Rover 800. In 1992 the range was boosted further by the addition of a Volvo-rivalling estate; offering Mercedes practicality for people with a lower budget.

Ford's intended replacement for the Granada Mk3 finally broke with tradition and adopted the Scorpio nameplate, but retained the new tradition of American styling. While the forthcoming Mercedes E-class might have taken inspiration from Marty Feldman and thus tempered the market response to bold styling, the huge headlamps and chromium Hollywood grin shifted the model from a car that meant business to one which resembled a joke. The melted chocolate plastics inside didn't help, while the slender rear lights of the saloon simply made it look like it had the backside of an elephant. If the Mk3's launch ten years earlier hadn't frightened customers off, the last hurrah for the big Ford would do the rest. ■

	Ford Granada Mk3 1.8	Ford Granada Mk3 2.0	Ford Granada Mk3 2.4	Ford Granada Mk3 2.5 diesel	Ford Granada/ Scorpio 2.8
CAPACITY	1796cc	1998cc	2393cc	2498cc	2792cc
POWER	90bhp	125bhp	130bhp	92bhp	150bhp
TORQUE	103lb.ft	128lb.ft	142lb.ft	150lb.ft	161lb.ft
TOP SPEED	107mph	114mph	122mph	107mph	127mph

Vauxhall Carlton and Senator

Vauxhall's finest would take on the Fords from the previous pages in the executive sector

The replacement of the FE series Vauxhalls with the Carlton, Viceroy and Senator had by and large been a success – even if the small six pot Viceroy had been a slow enough seller to be dropped in favour of a 2.2-litre facelift Carlton. The two model strategy recalled the Velox and Cresta top-line approach of the 1950s and 1960s, and was more successful for Vauxhall than pinning all its hopes on a single model that straddled market classes. It's thus entirely unsurprising that when the time came for Opel to replace the Rekord and Senator models with the new Omega and Senator B in 1986 and 1987 respectively, Vauxhall variants would soon follow. The new Carlton and new Senator were – in concept – more of the same, but both

models spawned performance variants that hit the headlines, making the children of big Vauxhall owners untouchably cool in the school playground.

The car every kid wished their dad would bring home was of

course the Lotus Carlton – a car so powerful that questions were asked about its legality in Parliament. Effectively, the Lotus Carlton was a Carlton 3000GSi, stroked out to 3.6 litres and fitted with a brace of turbochargers.

A six speed manual gearbox from the Chevrolet Corvette and lots of tweaks by the then GM-owned Lotus Cars made for a phenomenally quick supersaloon with genuine 175mph potential. It wasn't cheap; something

Carlton was a staple of the motorway service station.

Capacious carryalls rivalled Volvo for their ability to swallow any luggage.

Vauxhall acknowledged by loading it to the gunwales with kit including a walnut dash, leather seats, and exclusive Imperial Green paintwork. The popular kids might spout guff about cars like the Rover Vitesse and the Sierra Cosworth, but the ones who knew about cars knew that the little Lotus badge on the back of the big Vauxhall means a car that could have Ferraris quaking in their tyres.

By contrast, many kids spent their free time looking over their shoulder hopeful that their antics wouldn't land them in the back of a 24v Senator. Because there is still no more iconic area or traffic car than a Senator B with jam sandwich striping, a big blue light bar and that big chip-cutter grille hiding extra blues. You might have been lucky, your father might be a company director and have secured himself a Senator through service, but the majority of children who got to know the inside of a Senny were miscreants being taken home to explain their behaviour to their parents. For the parents themselves there was little scarier on a motorway than the looming presence of the big Vauxhall, and nothing

King of the hill was the Lotus Carlton, a car so outrageous it prompted questions in Parliament.

guaranteed to make you check your speed as quickly as a flash of its blue lights.

If you had a white Senator as a civilian, motorways became hunting grounds for some of the silliest sports imaginable – and the best part was, you didn't even have to do anything to prompt it. You could come up behind unsuspecting BMW drivers in the fast lane, flash your lights and watch them panic as they moved over while trying not to brake too quickly. Or you could stick to 60mph in the inside lane and snigger as the queue of desperately law abiding motorists built up behind you, none brave enough

Stretched Senator was the director's favourite.

Optional digital dashboard was up to the minute, but looks dated today.

an early GL, which came on some of the most mesmerising wheel trims of their era. Unlike everyone else, who had given in and fitted plastic, Vauxhall fitted brushed steel wheel trims that caught and reflected the light, meaning that in the right light a Carlton looked head and shoulders above the opposition. Or a 2.5 Senator – and while it was optional, even the entry level Senator could be had with the same sort of digital dashboard as the Vauxhall Astra GTE, meaning that even sober suited businessmen could pretend that they were in Knight Rider. And let's not forget that the 24v model's appeal to the police meant a high turnover of cheap white Sennies at auction once they reached about five years old, offering family men a lot of bang for their buck if they didn't mind the pared-down spec or the holes drilled in the dashboard. Later in the car's life the six pot made its way back into non sporting Carltons, reviving the Viceroy concept in all but name with cars like the Carlton Diplomat and Diamond. And at the other end of the spectrum there were efficient 2.3 litre diesel models targeted at the taxi market.

Vauxhall would replace the Carlton in 1993, giving in and using the Omega name from its Opel equivalent for the new model. The Senator's replacement, the Vauxhall Elite, shared the Omega's body and was believed by many to be a submodel. ∎

to risk overtaking what they thought to be Plod. Of course, wearing a suit – as you often would if your Senator was a company car – only made people even more convinced you were an undercover officer just waiting to book them.

These two cars were the halo models though, and most families were unlikely to have gone shopping with anything like the sort of budget needed to buy a Lotus – or to get hold of a 24v Senator in any way except a police disposal auction. More typical for the family man would be something like

One fleet buyer in particular loved the Senator...

	Vauxhall Carlton 1.8	Vauxhall Carlton 2.0i	Vauxhall Senator 3.0 12v	Vauxhall Senator 3.0 24v	Lotus Carlton
CAPACITY	1796cc	1996cc	2969cc	2969cc	3615cc
POWER	115bhp	122bhp	180bhp	202bhp	377bhp
TORQUE	111lb.ft	129lb.ft	183lb.ft	200lb.ft	419lb.ft
TOP SPEED	122mph	123mph	125mph	140mph	176mph

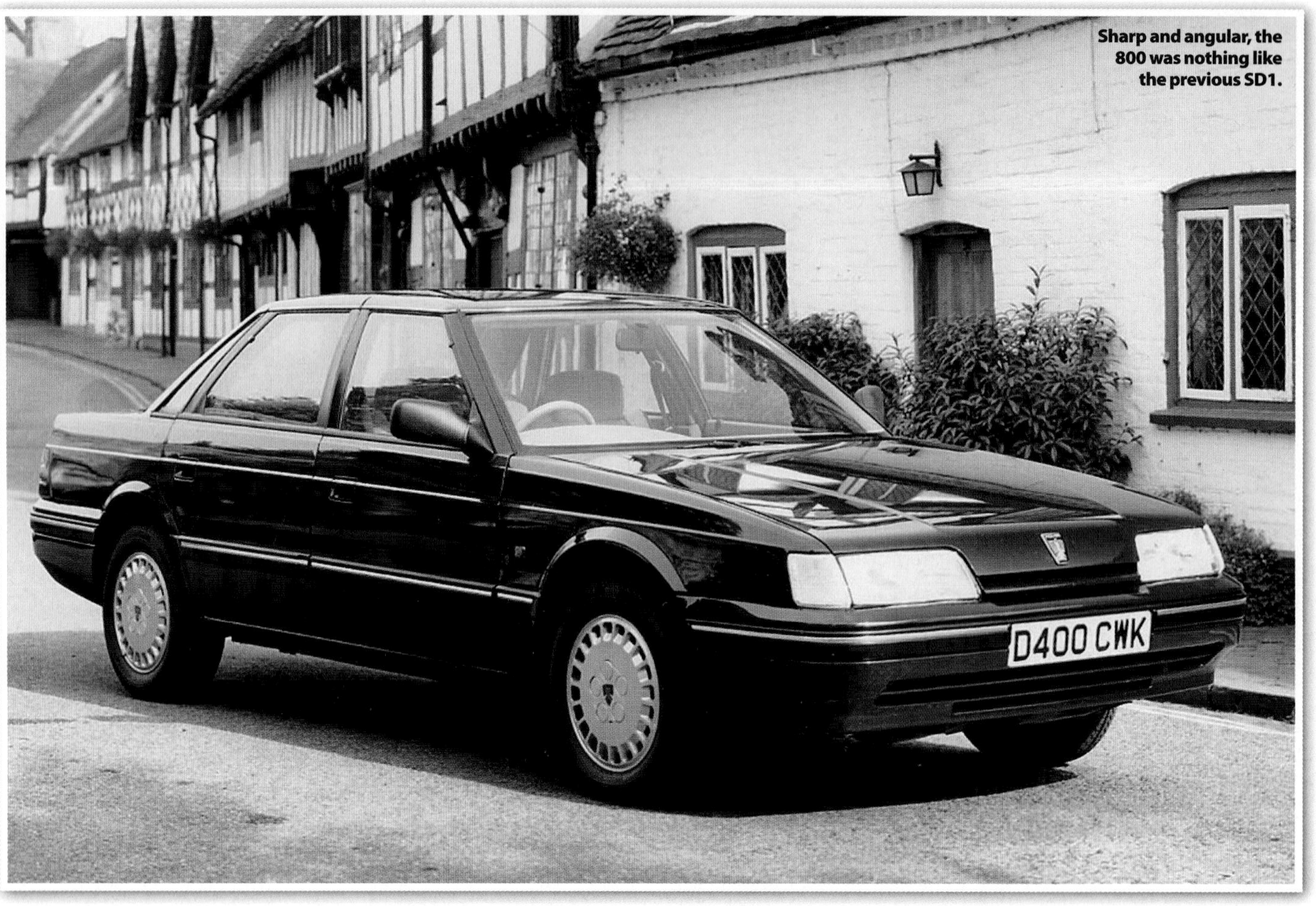

Sharp and angular, the 800 was nothing like the previous SD1.

rover 800

The result of Rover's first true collaboration with Honda was Britain's best-selling executive car.

We spoke about the Austin-Rover and Honda tie up back in the first section, where we discussed the Triumph Acclaim. And while that car was the first fruit of the joint venture, nobody was fooled – it was a Honda with new badges. The Rover 800 – and the Honda Legend -was the first real fruit of the joint venture, melding expertise from both Rover and Honda in a project which enabled both to fill gaps in their ranges with a jointly developed vehicle. The smaller engines and the aesthetics came from Rover, the V6 and the suspension came from Honda. Both manufacturers shared hard points, but had their own body panels.

And it was a relationship that on the surface showed so much promise. The Rover 800 of 1986 was sharply styled, felt upmarket, bristled with technology and – despite extensive Japanese input – felt British. It was a very different car to the SD1 that came before, but it spoke of its era and gave

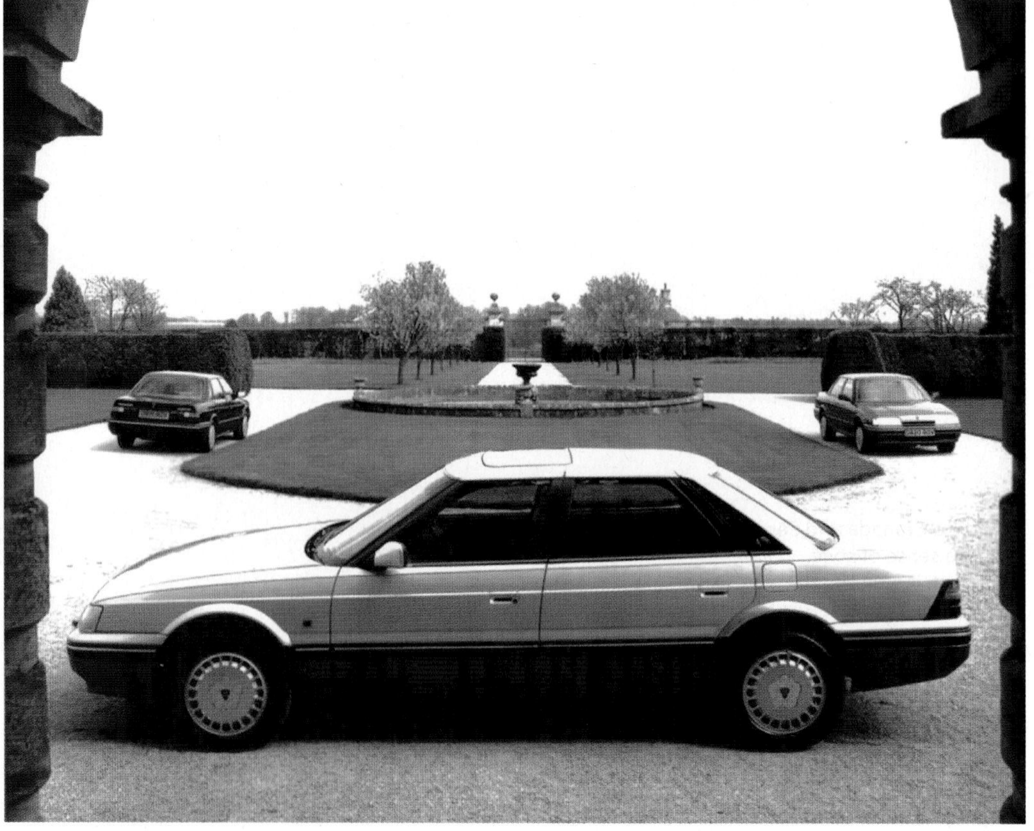

Two tone paintwork typically denoted range topping Sterling model.

would-be Granada and Senator buyers a sense of style.

At least, it did until the problems began. Electrical issues were rife in those early cars, along with poor plastics – and the early 2.5 litre V6 was all but lacking in torque. Efforts to market the car in American as the Sterling 825SL – the Rover name having been irrevocably tainted by the SD1 – went about as well as you would expect; sharp edged styling and impressive discounts couldn't distract attention from yawning dashboards that turned green in the sun, and American buyers simply bought exactly the same package in trusted Honda guise in the form of the Acura Legend instead.

Back in Britain, the cachet the Rover name still held meant that the car sold well. And in fairness, beyond its issues there was a good car there – the 800 was handsome, spacious, and the 2.0 versions at least went well. The range was boosted further for 1988 with the fitment of a larger 2.7 litre version of the V6 which went some way toward allaying concerns over torque, and with the introduction of a new fastback variant that met the needs of former SD1 buyers better than a saloon. Top of the new fastback range was the Vitesse; a half-leather trimmed bahnstormer that – despite a much more sanitised image – was actually faster in the real world than the V8 Vitesse it replaced. Children of a certain age will no doubt remember Rover's record attempt; setting a lap time in the hands of Tony Pond around the Isle of Man TT circuit. The Rover 827 Vitesse held that record for well over a decade, only being beaten

by a modified Subaru Impreza WRX in the post-millennium years. While it might have lacked the shove of the Saab 9000 Turbo or the everyman image of the Sierra Cosworth, this was real performance cred that its competitors simply couldn't match. At boardroom level there was the Sterling; a Vanden Plas by another name offering leather and electric rear seats as standard. There was even a limited run 820 Turbo for 1991; previewing the Mk2 Vitesse with 180bhp and a special bodykit by Tickford as a cut-price alternative to the Vitesse V6.

Most families though will have experienced the car in Si or SLi trim. Your writer's formative years were spent in the back seat of a decade-old Stone Grey 827SLi – handsome, quick, but with plenty of the quality issues we mentioned above. My nursery-age sister managed to pull the wood trim from the rear doors while strapped into her child seat, the radio never worked, and the car ultimately died of a cracked block.

The 1991 facelift looked much more imposing, but managed to miss the mark. In a bid to pander to the Sterling division in America, a two-door coupe was developed and the suspension across the range softened to turn the car into a boulevard cruiser. Unfortunately, short travel suspension does not a wafter make, and Rover ended up with a car that could be crashy and wobbly at the same time. To add insult to injury, before the Mk2 could be launched Rover pulled out of the American market for good, saddling the world with a car specified to appeal in a market that it would never see. The very last cars are arguably the most special feeling – fitted with Rover's new KV6 engine in

the post-Honda era, in the right colour they hide their 1980s origins well. It could have been better still though; the facelift was designed to allow for the reuse of MK1 doors and roof to save tooling, only for Rover to find its tooling worn beyond repair just before the launch of the new models. It was thus forced to retool; saving no money as a result of its design compromises.

Rover replaced the 800 – along with the smaller 600 – with the new 75 in 1998. A smaller and much more traditional car, it was clearly aimed at a very different

Vitesse model set records on the Isle of Man TT circuit.

1988 saw the launch of the fastback, here in 827Si form.

type of buyer. But by then, the executive car market had changed in the culmination of a process that had really begun in the 1980s. Buyers in the late-1990s and the 2000s favoured smaller cars by manufacturers perceived to be more premium – Ford also gave up on the Granada, and Vauxhall on its largest models. The traditional buyers of large cars from mainstream manufacturers had shifted into buyers of smaller BMW, Mercedes and Audi models, sacrificing the luxury of extra space in favour of extra street cred. ■

Basic 820 used the engine from the Austin Montego to create a spiritual Ambassador successor.

	Rover 820	Rover 820e	Rover 820Si	Rover 825i	Rover Vitesse 2.7	Rover 820 Turbo
CAPACITY	1994cc	1994cc	1994cc	2494cc	2675cc	1994cc
POWER	104bhp	118bhp	134bhp	165bhp	177bhp	180bhp
TORQUE	120lb.ft	119lb.ft	131lb.ft	163lb.ft	168lb.ft	159lb.ft
TOP SPEED	115mph	118mph	125mph	127mph	134mph	137mph

Saab 900 Turbos were the domain of the intellectual and off-beat buyer.

saab 900

One of the more unusual family offerings of the era, but also one of the most sensible

The Saab 900 is one of those cars that's never quite fitted in. It's never quite looked like anything else, never quite behaved like anything else, never really appealed to anybody except a traditional Saab enthusiast. Saab was turbocharging cars before almost anyone else, offering unusual performance-led family saloons that were well-built yet different. It was never the car your parents owned and never the car that your best mate's dad was given by his boss; it was the car your eccentric uncle might have taken you to the pictures in or the car your neighbour who worked for an aerospace company might have driven while your dad owned a Sierra or a Granada. The car that the weird kid in school had on his bedroom wall, rather than that tennis poster or a Ferrari. That sense of otherworldliness, that sense of exoticness is the thing that means we remember the 900 so well – that and the fact that with production stretching from 1979 to 1993, it was the car that outlasted the decade we all associate it with the most.

Five door models offered more practicality, but gawky looks.

There was always the feeling growing up, that people had to be deliberately contrary to find a Saab appealing. The lines were never quite coherent, the proportions ever so slightly off – it was a car that seemed to thrive on its anti-image image and a car that nobody ever seemed to consider buying unless it was very definitely what they wanted. No list of prospective purchases ever included the line "or a Saab 900". If it had competition at all, it came in the forms of the Citroën CX and the Audi 100 – offbeat machinery that appealed to intellectuals, but not really cars that did the same thing…

But much of what made a 900 so unusual was also what made it so great as family transport for those open minded enough – and well enough off – to have considered one. The 900 was narrow, an odd boast until you remember that Bristol deliberately made narrower GTs to appeal to city dwellers for

Long tail hid a floor-height boot sill for ease of loading.

whom extra width was a bad thing. The 900 was long, longer than its supposed big brother the 9000, which in turn meant it had a big boot. The hatchback models had a completely flat floor and a floor level loading height, so heavy objects could be accommodated with ease. The 900 was quick enough in all guises – yet because all 900s came with 2.0 four pots

they weren't expensive to run. People always said spares were expensive, but the truth was it was no more costly than a Cavalier to service. And not only were there spaces left on the dashboard for switches for extra accessories, Saab even sold "Extra" switches with which to fit them.

So it was a well-considered car that appealed to people who put thought into their purchases.

But there was another side to Saab – one which had begun in the 1970s with the 99 Turbo. Saab wanted a larger engine, and having ruled out a V8 it turned to forced induction as a way to get more bang from the 2.0 unit shared with the Triumph Dolomite range. Suddenly one of the more offbeat premium cars was also one of the fastest, and Saab was glad to continue this trend with

the newer, larger 900. It became the yuppie car for people who didn't want to be thought of as yuppies; red brace transport for people who'd rather wear a nice sensible belt. What really started to get people talking about the 900 Turbo in terms of image was the James Bond association; the continuation books approved by Ian Fleming's estate put Britain's favourite secret agent behind the

Impractical headgear perhaps, but the 900 convertible was the ultimate style accessory.

Clever integral spoiler helped to hide the roof when folded.

wheel of a tricked out 900 that had nothing to do with Q-Branch, but which was his own choice of car. Suddenly Saabs were starting to look cool, a shift that only intensified when Saab introduced a convertible variant. Developed to appease the American market (which had always rather appreciated the oddball nature of the marque), the convertible made conventional four seaters such as the BMW 3-series convertible look dull and old hat at a stroke. Not only that but it was a convertible you could enjoy in all weathers – the hood worked for wet days, and the heater was like a blast furnace for those sunny days in minus temperatures. Heated seats on most, too.

While few families might have had a new Saab, moving toward the end of the decade they made surprisingly popular used family cars because all the magazines said the right things. Saabs tended to be solid, well made, well looked after, and owned by the sort of people you could trust. They might have been more expensive even used than a Ford or a Vauxhall, but they were the sort of car you would buy and keep for several years safe in the knowledge that nothing would ever go wrong. And they were the sort of car that attracted repeat business – if you ever managed to wear out a 900 you'd go and buy another one.

It's not surprising that today the 900 is a cult classic – not only a car to cosset and cherish, but a car that's just as capable of serving as family transport almost fifty years on. Moreover, it's appealing to a whole new generation of families today – the children of 900 drivers are still using and enjoying the cars themselves. How many of the cars in these pages instil such brand loyalty, even a decade after the manufacturer closed its doors? ■

	Saab 900	Saab 900i	Saab 900 Turbo	Saab 900 Turbo 16
CAPACITY	1985cc	1985cc	1985cc	1985cc
POWER	100bhp	110bhp	145bhp	175bhp
TORQUE	111lb.ft	119lb.ft	174lb.ft	195lb.ft
TOP SPEED	105mph	105mph	119mph	125mph

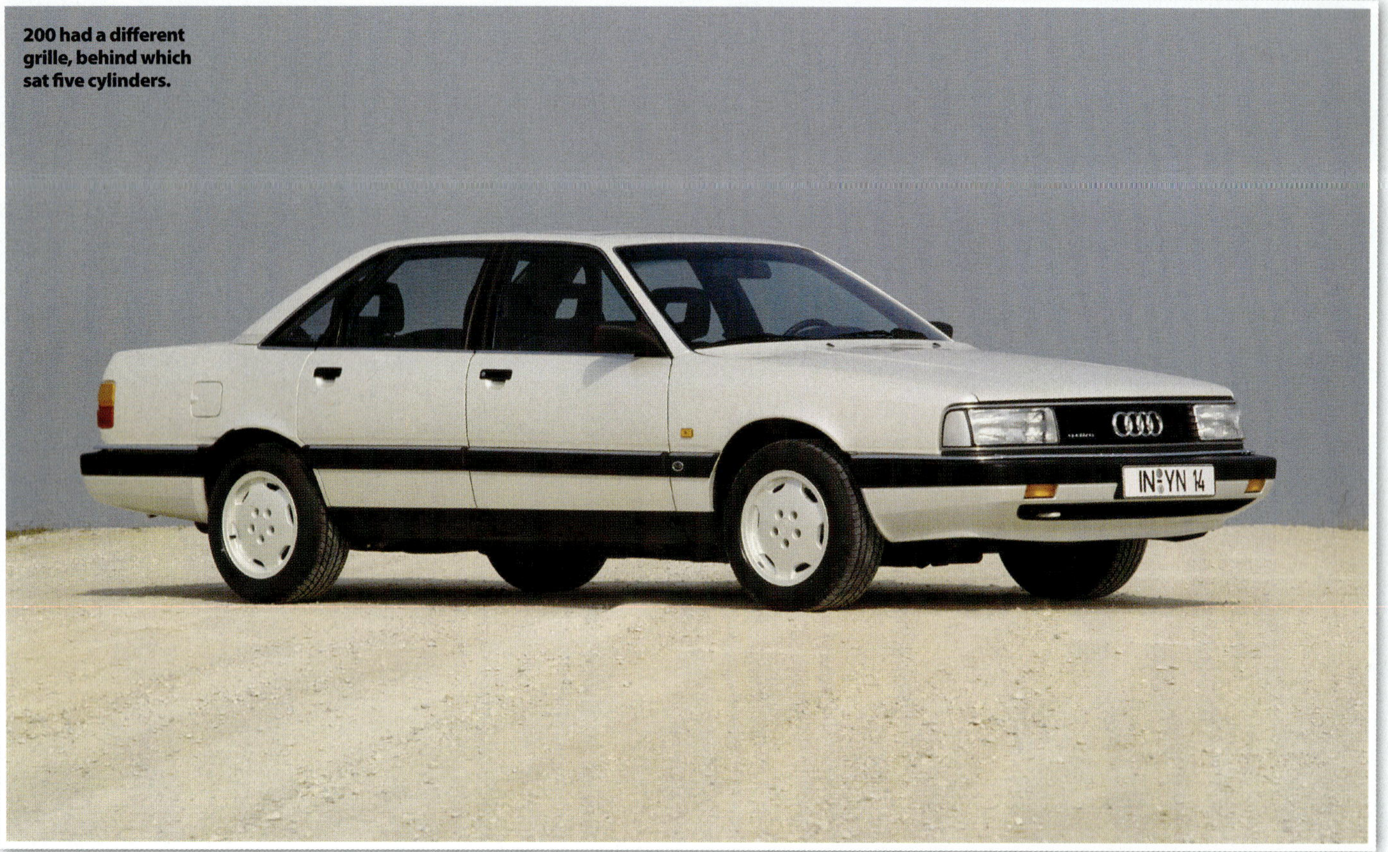

200 had a different grille, behind which sat five cylinders.

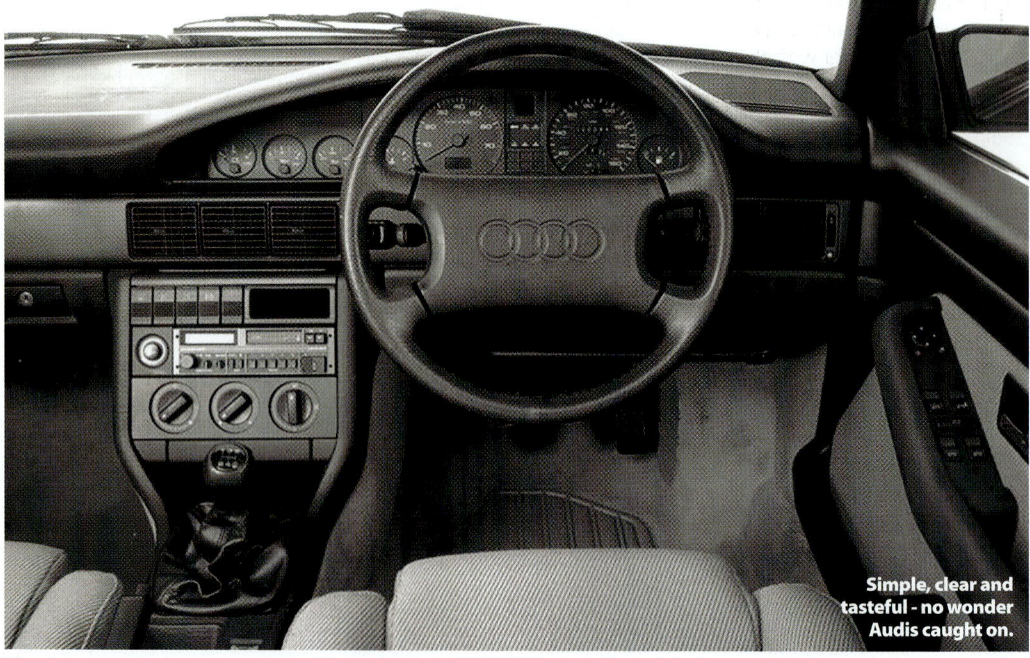

Audi 100 and 200

Swish and aerodynamic, the 100 for the 1980s was the car that made Audi truly cool.

If you wanted to get on the beach before the Germans, you needed an Audi 100. We all knew it, Geoffrey Palmer said so on the telly. And while the ad was a thinly veiled wisecrack about national stereotypes and sun loungers, the fact remained that the 100 really did set new standards in terms of executive car design. Cosmetically it harked back to its old rotary-engined sibling, the NSU Ro80, but built upon its clean and modern lines with such niceties as flush fitting glass and aerodynamic wheel trims. These meant that the 100 was slippery and wind cheating, and its efficient engines made the competition look profligate with its petrol.

It kickstarted a new attitude toward not only Audi, but the executive car sector as a whole. Those four rings on the bonnet went from a denoter of staid but reliable upmarket Volkswagens to marking a car with real design flair. It might have shared its engines with the Golf and the Passat but the Audi 100 was a class apart – larger and more advanced than the competition from BMW and Mercedes while remaining better value than both, it was the car that made the motoring press sit up and take notice. And while there were certainly clever and more futuristic executive saloons of the period, the Audi was the real trend setter. Look at the roads of Britain today – every second car is German from a premium manufacturer, everything aerodynamic and slick – it was Audi that first showed us the way we could have it, and arguably Audi which kickstarted the drive through the 1980s and 1990s

Simple, clear and tasteful - no wonder Audis caught on.

away from the mainstream brands and into aspirational, premium metal.

The 100 was the start of a new push for the German company – when married to Audi's famed five-cylinder engine, it begat the upmarket 200 model with nicer trim, a slightly different not and an optional turbocharger. Further down the range, there was a new 80 for 1986, and a new 90 the year after with the five-pot under the bonnet. This was the era in which it became cool to drive an Audi – and each and every model had the option of the Quattro all wheel drive system made famous on the rally stages of the world. The sort of people who bought Audis were those who valued solidity and strong engineering and who were canny with the purse strings; we know of at least one Concorde engineer who spent the 1980s behind the wheel of a succession of 100s and they weren't the only examples in the car park at Filton. If you appreciated the qualities of a Mercedes-Benz but didn't want to show off then the Audi 100 was a perfect alternative. If the 100 saloon was right up your street but you needed to carry the occasional sideboard or husky, there was a 100 Avant too – unlike its predecessor, this generation of Avant was a fully fledged estate car and one which came with its very own echo. Gone was the need to buy a Volvo if you couldn't afford the Mercedes estate; the Audi 100 Avant offered exactly the same stylish image and even more space for a much smaller sum. Entirely unsurprisingly the driveways of public schools and Surrey stable yards soon swelled to the seams with rows of parked Avants, and it became THE carry-all in which to be seen.

And it wasn't all about the image either. While Audi 100s were front wheel drive, the engine was mounted longitudinally which helped with the weight balance, and if was derived from the same basic engine fitted to the VW Golf GTi. The 100 had great seats and a clearly laid out dashboard, and the Mercedes comparisons didn't just stop in the brochures – the build quality was very nearly to Stuttgart standards. While standard equipment was Germanically meagre, it was possible to spec your 100 up with leather, air conditioning, alloy

AUDI 100 AND 200

Optional quattro all wheel drive made the 100 grippy in winter.

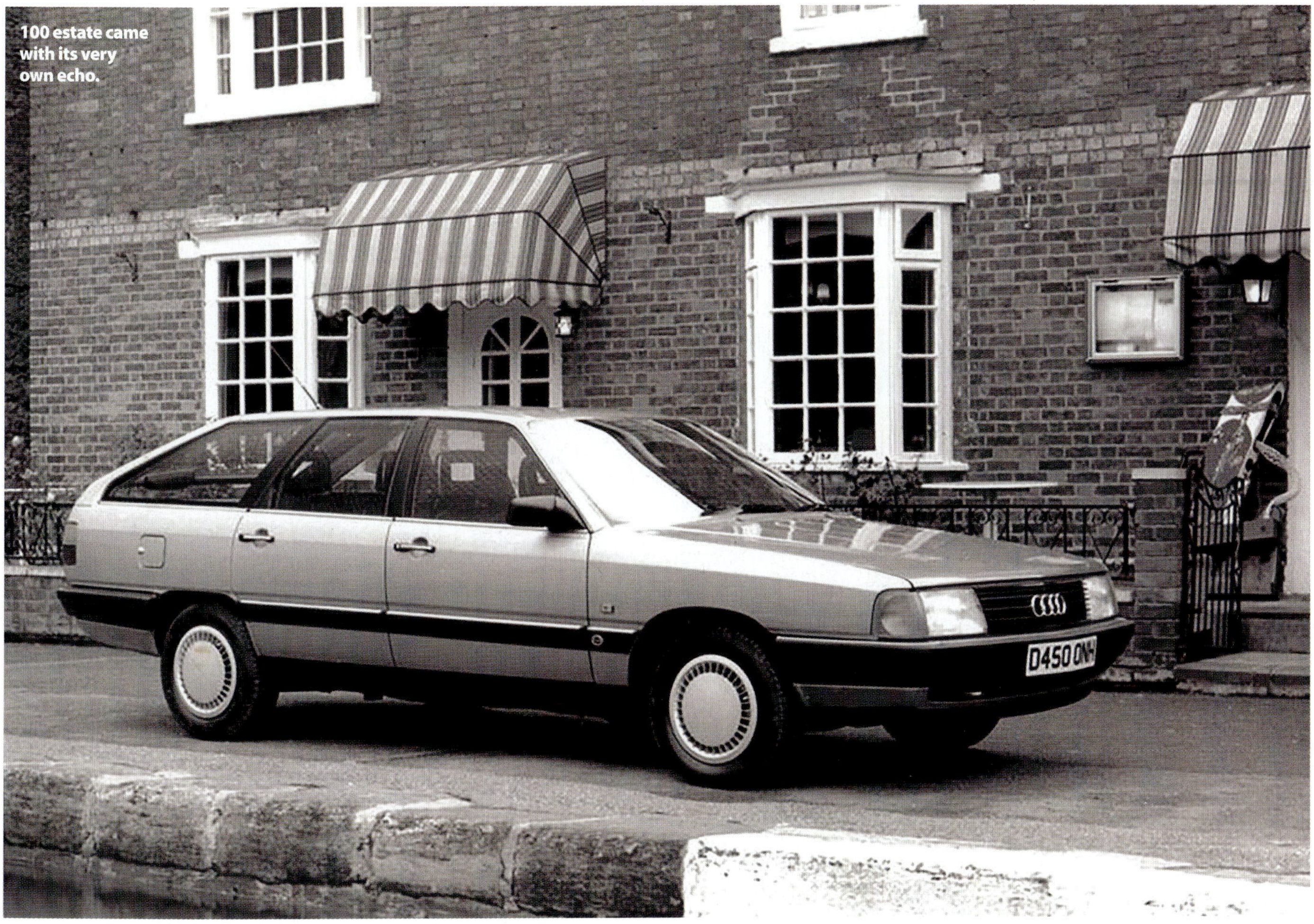

100 estate came with its very own echo.

	Audi 100CD	Audi 100 2.3E	Audi 100 quattro	Audi 200 Turbo
CAPACITY	2144cc	2226cc	2226cc	1994cc
POWER	136bhp	138bhp	138bhp	182bhp
TORQUE	133lb.ft	139lb.ft	139lb.ft	259lb.ft
TOP SPEED	129mph	122mph	119mph	145mph

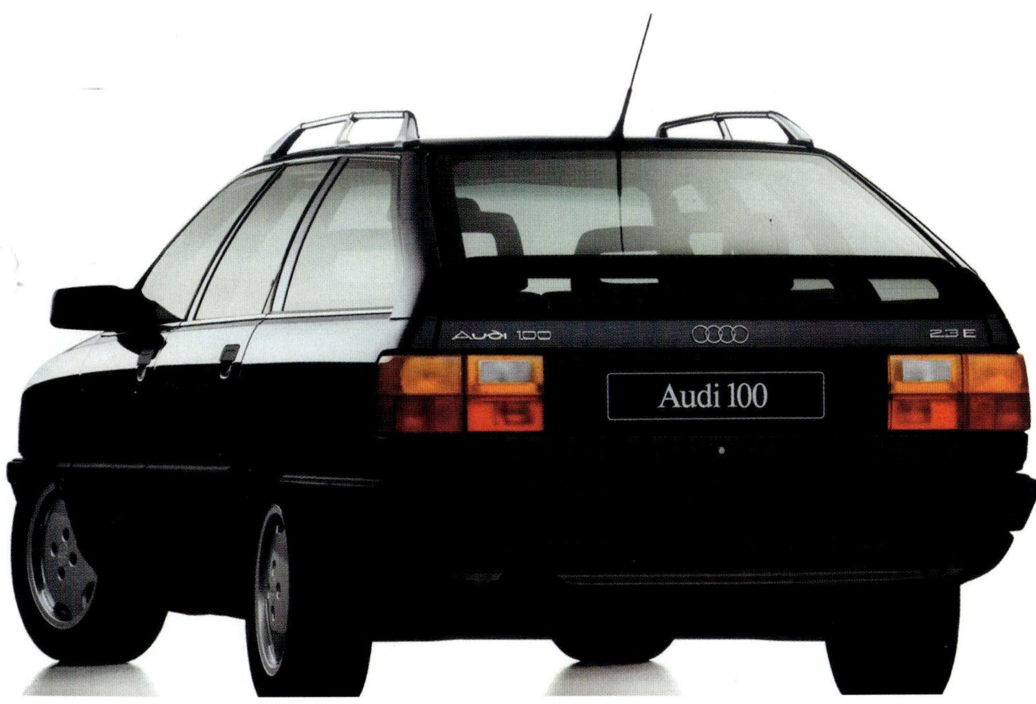

wheels and a nice Blaupunkt radio, all of which came as standard on the five cylinder 200 versions. Those got the five cylinder engine seen in the Quattro, so while there was a little more weight over the nose which affected the handling, there was more performance and it sounded cool in that sort of off beat warbly way familiar to anybody who watched the RAC Rally on the television.

But if all that wasn't enough, Audi even had a final trump card to play for the family man who wanted it all. Because the Audi 100 was one of the first cars to be offered on sale in the UK with a galvanised body. So while your Rover 800 or Ford Granada would start turning ferrous at the edges the day it left the showroom and stone chips could become automotive acne almost overnight, the big Audi stayed blister and blemish free well into middle age. People buying these cars as cheaper family transport even a decade and a half later – when there was no bigger or better two grand saloon available – could expect their cars to look as good as the day they were new. Audi's slogan of Vorsprung Durch Technik – ahead through technology – has scarcely found a better home. ■

The 25 was styled by Robert Opron, who also did the Citroën SM

Renault 25 GTX

renault 25

Overlooked in favour of almost every other executive car, was the Renault 25 unfairly forgotten?

Didn't you hate those two yuppies? The man and his wife on the Renault 25 advert. Having just dropped off their daughter for a violin lesson, Mr Hero starts what sounds like a difficult conversation with his wife. Something she ought to know, concerning the house, the kids… it's time for him to go it alone. Yes, that's right, he's starting his own business. The bank has given him the backing, and some of his colleagues are ready to jump into the unknown with him. The only thing is, he's got to give up the company car. Wifey is not best pleased, despite the look of faint relief on our hero's face. "One of your better decisions" read the advertising strapline - after the only decision we saw our man take was the one to give the Renault 25 V6 back to his old bosses.

It isn't, perhaps, unfair of us to wonder whether the car might have been the final straw for

Even by executive standards, the interior was plush.

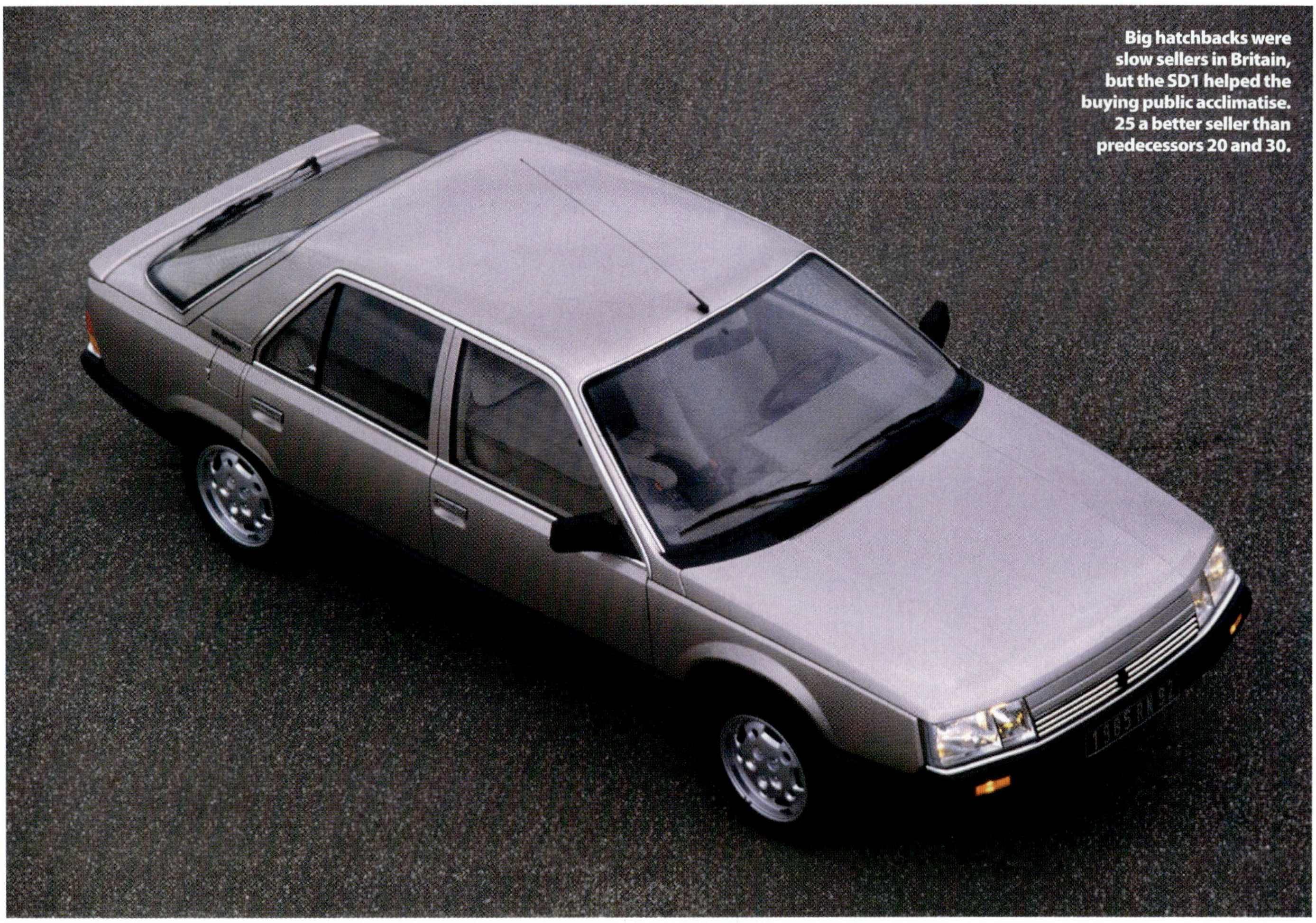

Big hatchbacks were slow sellers in Britain, but the SD1 helped the buying public acclimatise. 25 a better seller than predecessors 20 and 30.

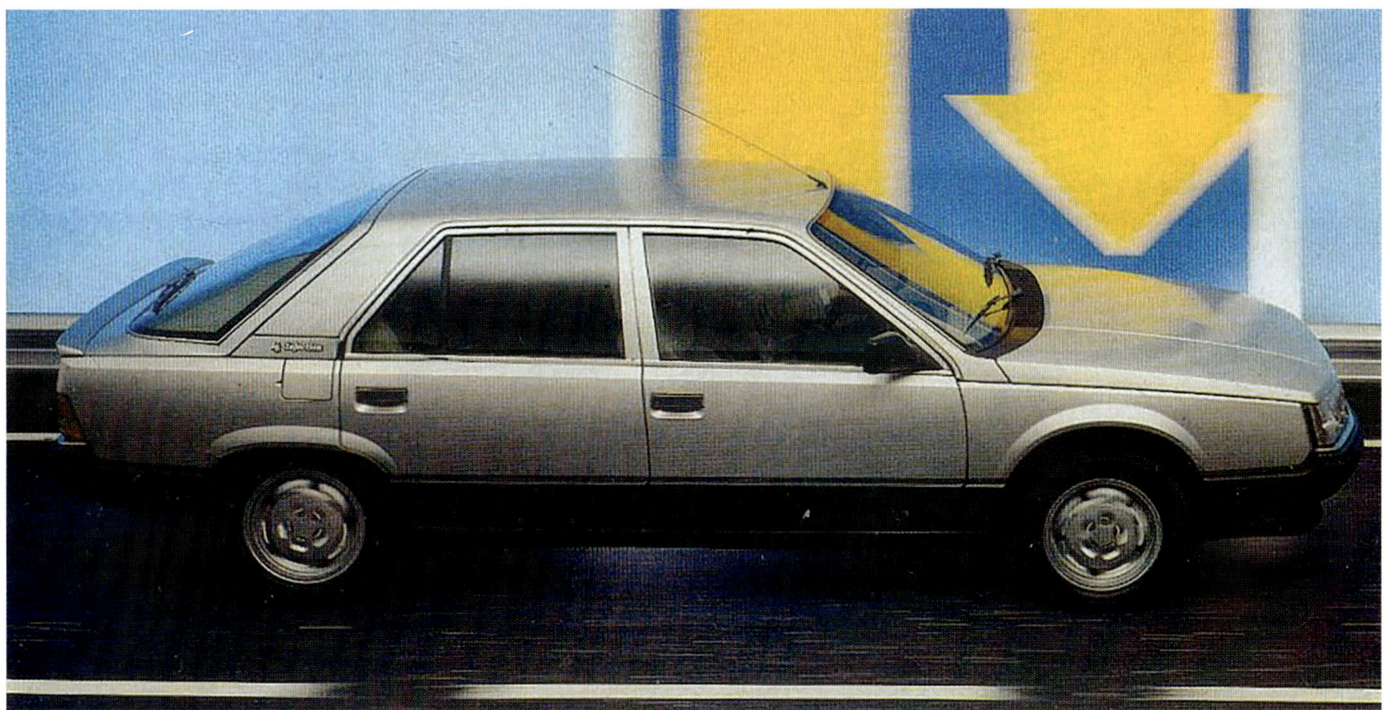

him. Because at £14800 the 25 was up against some formidable alternatives that would have been much more imposing on the driveway. The company could have stretched to one of the new shape Mercedes-Benz 230Es for instance, or a BMW 528i, or if he needed the hatchback he could have had a Rover SD1 3500 Vanden Plas. If it was a French firm and needed to give its management French cars, it could have indulged him with the unconventionally brilliant Citroën CX25 GTi Turbo. Ultimately, the biggest problem that the Renault 25 had in the British market was that there was simply no reason to buy one.

But if you could ignore the awful, awful couple on the television ads and really wanted to buy a car nobody else had, the Renault 25 wasn't a bad choice. Popular in its native France among patriots and politicians, the Renault 25 was as comfortable as your favourite armchair and – if you bought a posh one – had just as many buttons as your nice new hifi. Like the hifi, there was even a graphic equaliser if you paid enough. While the ride in the equally French Citroën was unbeatable, the Renault rode incredibly well for conventional springs and dampers and its seats ran rings around the majority of the opposition. The Renault was also a hatchback; too – the company that invented the concept arguably gave us the

Top spec Baccara came with walnut trim, and a graphic equaliser to ensure that yes Sir, its occupants could boogie.

most stylish and useful executive hatchback of the decade; the Rover 800 being a little derivative and the Mk3 Granada just plain boring. Robert Opron, when styling the 25, was in some ways looking to evoke the work he did with the 1970s Citroën SM supercar – wrap around glass, a prominent rear pillar and rectangular lighting blending well with the established Renault themes of the decade to create a car that looked bang up to date and yet vaguely futuristic at the same time.

And with space for five six footers in comfort, it was big even for a car of its class. They sat in an interior styled by Marcello Gandini in the down-time between Lamborghini sketches, surrounded by all the best that the decade could offer. There was ample space for luggage, too, making the 25 one of the best cross-continental cruisers a family could wish for. If you had long distance family or liked to drive to the continent for your holidays there were few finer cars capable of carrying the kids.

For 1988, Renault introduced a top spec model, filled with walnut and leather and stuffed to the gunwales with toys – based on the V6, with a V6 Turbo option from 1991. Great concept – making one of the most comfortable cars on the road

25s can still be found in regular use in their home country of France.

even more refined and upmarket would go down well, even if the Renault badge didn't endear it to company car choosers from the off. But just as nobody today would drive around in a Nissan Qashqai Bruno Mars, a Range Rover Jedward or a Cupra Leon Tulisa, the idea of driving around in a Renault 25 Baccara was understandably difficult to sell to the sort of person otherwise used to Senators, Sterlings and Scorpios. Yes Sir, I Can Boogie wasn't quite the right message to give to your clients in the company car park… The limited edition Monaco made much more sense from an image perspective – like the smaller Renault Monacos, the 25 came in metallic Oak Bronze paint with tan leather and alloy wheels. It might only have had the entry level 2.0 engine and it might have been based on the entry level GTS spec, but that didn't matter; it had separate front centre armrests for the driver and passenger and a graphic equaliser.

Renault replaced the 25 with the Safrane in 1992 – by which UK sales had slowed even further. A facelift in 1988 had made the 25 look like a big Renault 19, but this anodynisation only made the model even more forgettable to the buying public. The only people in the UK who remember the 25 even existed are those lucky enough to have experienced it, because it was one of the best-kept automotive secrets of its era. ∎

	Renault 25 TXi	Renault 25 V6	Renault 25 V6 Turbo
CAPACITY	1995cc	2664cc	2458cc
POWER	140bhp	142bhp	182bhp
TORQUE	130lb.ft	162lb.ft	207lb.ft
TOP SPEED	128mph	130mph	139mph

Facelift softened some of those sharper edges.

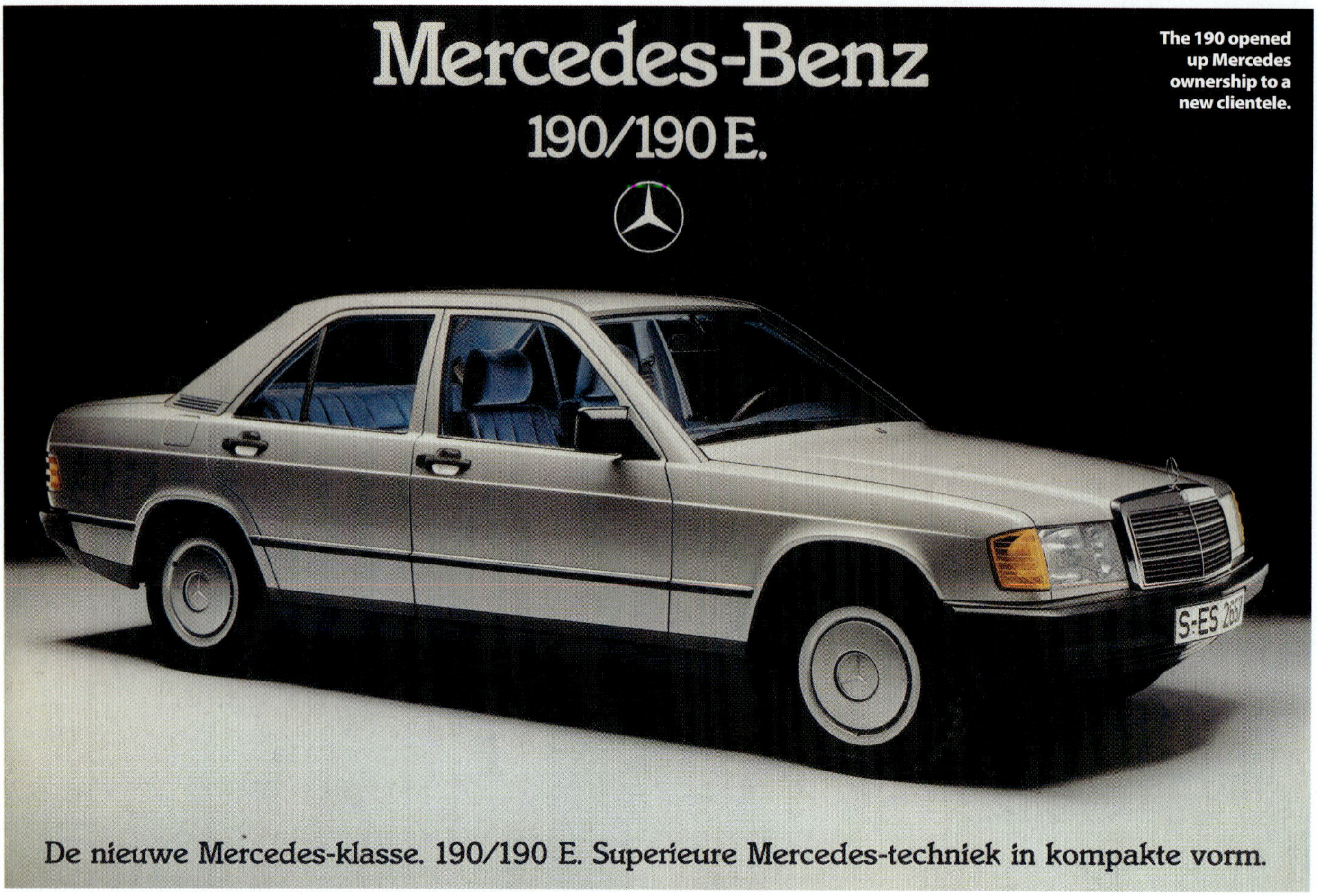

The 190 opened up Mercedes ownership to a new clientele.

slower sellers – executive expresses

We don't have space to give every family classic its own section in this title. Here are some of the best of the rest in the premium sector.

The biggest news for the family car buyer with a big chunk of cash to spend in the early 1980s came from Germany. Because while Mercedes had long appealed to the wealthier parts of middle class Britain for its strength, solidity and cast iron image, even the basic 200 was beyond the reach even of many company management types. From 1982, however, Mercedes had a new model to offer – the 190. Smaller than the 200, using the same 2.0 engines in carburetted and injected forms, the new car had the BMW 3-series firmly in its sights. Bigger, better engineered and equally sparsely equipped, it was a proper Mercedes that you could buy for Granada money. Complaints about power were soon

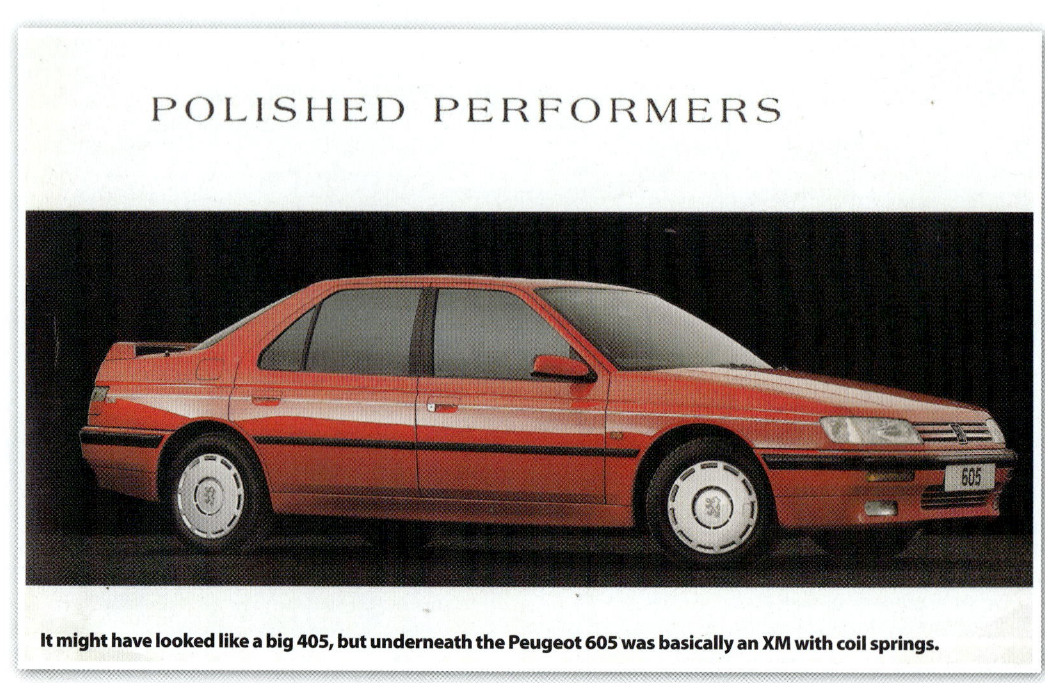

It might have looked like a big 405, but underneath the Peugeot 605 was basically an XM with coil springs.

The 1980s saw Bentley regain its independence.

addressed with the introduction of a Cosworth-tuned M3-baiter and a silky smooth 2.6 V6, but as you could buy a Jaguar for the cost of either they weren't common sights in 1980s Britain. Sales of the basic 2.0 variants stayed healthy, however, making the 190E Britain's best-selling Benz in the 1980s. And with few changes over its life, buyers in the late 1980s could buy secondhand examples, add a cheap personal plate and look like they were doing far better than they really were.

British buyers looked at the 190E 2.6 and thought it too small for the money – choosing something more flash for the cash. Typically that might be an entry level, 2.9 litre XJ40 – a car stuffed with technology. Instead of looking to its traditional client base and steering clear, Jaguar stole a sideways glance at the Aston Martin Lagonda and thought "We can do that too", and launched the XJ40 era of XJ6 in 1986. The XJ40 eschewed Jaguar's soft curves for square edges, and replaced the London club interior with something straight out of Tron. Well, if Tron had been set in a leather lined world of walnut, anyway. Buyers who craved the old world atmosphere could still buy the old model with the V12 engine, as Jaguar had deliberately designed the new car in such a way that it wouldn't fit – so legend tells us. The two models would continue side by side well into the 1990s, with SIII V12 and XJ40 3.6 Sovereign models setting their buyers back similar money. An interesting strategy, in that those scared off by tech could cower behind the wheel of a trad Jag, while those who felt the Series XJs old hat could step into the future instead.

Citroën XM and its Peugeot 605 sibling less unconventional than before.

Saab 9000 was part of a Swedish-Italian joint venture.

Or if those buyers had lottery wins behind them, they could buy one of the most historically important large saloons of the early 1980s. When Rolls-Royce has bought Bentley in the 1930s it effectively emasculated what was once a fiercely sporting brand, turning it into what Rolls-Royce dubbed the Silent Sports Car, which basically meant a coachbuilt Rolls-Royce – and from the 1950s onwards, the grille was the only real difference. 1983 changes that. While the new Mulsanne Turbo was still a Rolls-Royce with a different grille, but that grille was now painted rather than chromed. Under the bonnet sat a turbocharger the size of Cheshire, meaning that the marque could once again reclaim the title bestowed upon older Bentleys by Ettore Bugatti; the fastest lorries in the world. Explosive performance meant that the chassis was overburdened though, and the tighter Turbo R would assume the mantle of the fastest Bentley model from 1985 onwards.

1985 also saw a facelift of one of the most daring cars of the 1970s, the Citroën CX. Still ahead of its time in terms of its ride, handling and comfort, the CX with its heavy chrome bumpers

Citroën CX showed the executive sector it could be bold.

British buyers took the Jaguar XJ40 to their hearts.

and big flat wheel trims was starting to look like a product of the previous age. A facelift and new dashboard by Brit Geoff Matthews would change that; conventional dials and plastic bumpers tempered the madness while a radio mounted where the handbrake ought to live and an advertisement featuring Grace Jones's giant steel head strengthened the lunacy. It was enough to see the model through to 1989 – or 1991 in the form of the Safari estate – and the launch of its successor. The XM might have shared a platform with the forthcoming Peugeot 605, but the two cars couldn't be more different. The XM was a hatchback with an additional internal rear window to prevent draughts via the tailgate, a wedgy body with more than a hint of the SM supercar, and space for five in some of the softest seats this side of DFS. With the efficient and refined new 2.1 diesel under the bonnet it would swiftly become the car you hoped arrived for the airport taxi run.

Between this pair and Fiat's Type Four program, six European manufacturers effectively had the mid range executive sector sewn up. Because under the skin the Saab 9000, Lancia Thema, Fiat Croma and Alfa 164 had more in common than their dealers might be willing to admit, with three cars sharing key panels to boot. Of the four the Saab was always the strongest seller in Britain – a big upmarket hatch with a turbocharged engine – though the swish Pininfarina styling of the Alfa turned more than a few heads.

One often overlooked entry into the executive sector from Japan was the Nissan Maxima – a car that was so badly overlooked from its launch in Britain in 1989 that its successor, the Nissan QX, was marketed under the slogan "It Exists". People simply didn't know that about the Maxima which had come before – and with the exception of the airport trade, people had ignored the Laurel that came before that. Fitted with a 3.0 V6, the Maxima was targeted at the sort of family man who wanted a Honda Legend or Toyota Camry, but craved anonymity and felt that both of those options were simply too extrovert. After all, the Legend – co-developed with the Rover 800 – could be had not only as a sober suited four door saloon, but a rakish two door coupe. What madness was this?! ∎

Mondeo put an end to Ford's laziness, and swiftly became the market leader.

into the 1990s

The next decade would see considerable changes in the sorts of family cars people bought.

On the face of it, the 1990s were an era of positivity in Britain. Coming out of the end of the 1980s, there was a greater perception of wealth but behind the veneer of social conscience. Greed was no longer the byword, and people were reaping the benefits of arguably the best financial era since before the war. The Cold War was over, Springsteen had sung atop the Berlin Wall, and back home, a new era of Cool Britannia was being ushered in amid the melodies of Britpop. But some things never change, and they included our attitudes to our cars. Families still needed transport, and those families who grew up in the 1990s now look back fondly at an era in which cars had mostly become reliable, rot resistant and yet simple enough to be easy and cheap to maintain. Were the 1990s secretly the halcyon years of post war motoring? Some of the cars we loved back then make us think that maybe, it was.

Rover 200 and its 400 sister were a cut above Escort, Astra and Golf.

We cannot think of family cars of the 1990s without considering the car that arguably changed the rep sector forever: the Ford Mondeo. While there had been family saloons that were engaging to drive in the past – Peugeot 405, we're looking at you – the fact that Ford had the best fleet deals and the best dealer network meant that most reps and family men were doomed to spend their motoring hours behind the wheel of the Sierra. Ford's first true World Car was different – it went well, handled well, and was practical. No wonder Mondeo Man was the target of New Labour's third way – if you're selling a new future,

sell it to those who've never had it so good.

The Mondeo even – mostly – made up for Ford's previous disaster. If people hadn't been happy when the rear wheel drive Escort Mk2 was replaced with the front wheel drive Mk3, the Mk5 of 1990 was a new low. It felt like a cynical attempt to

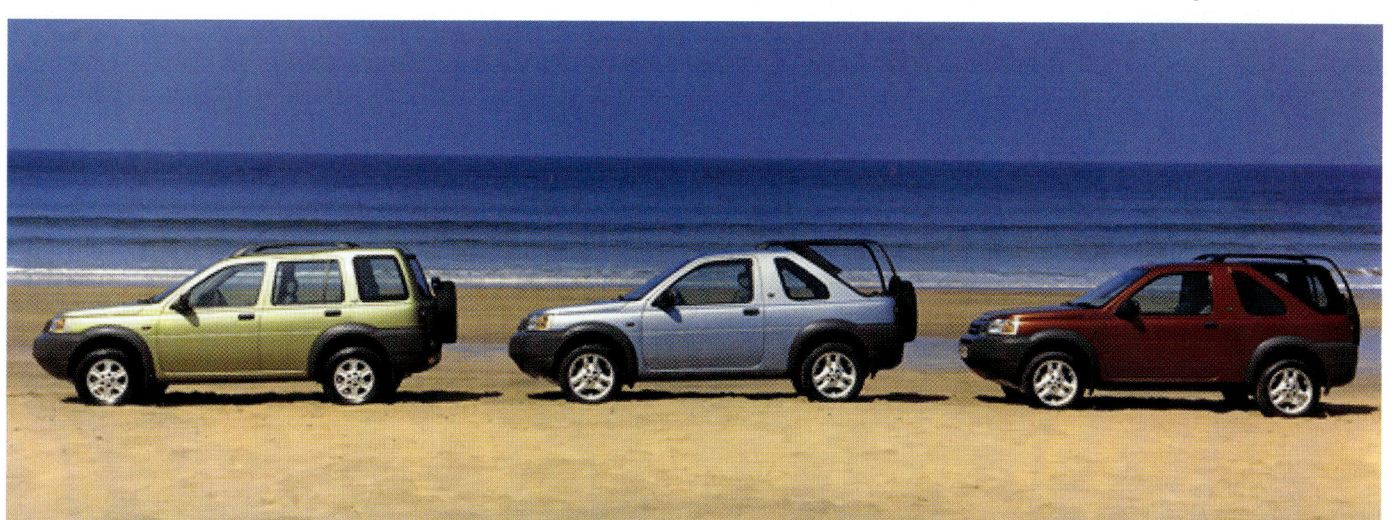

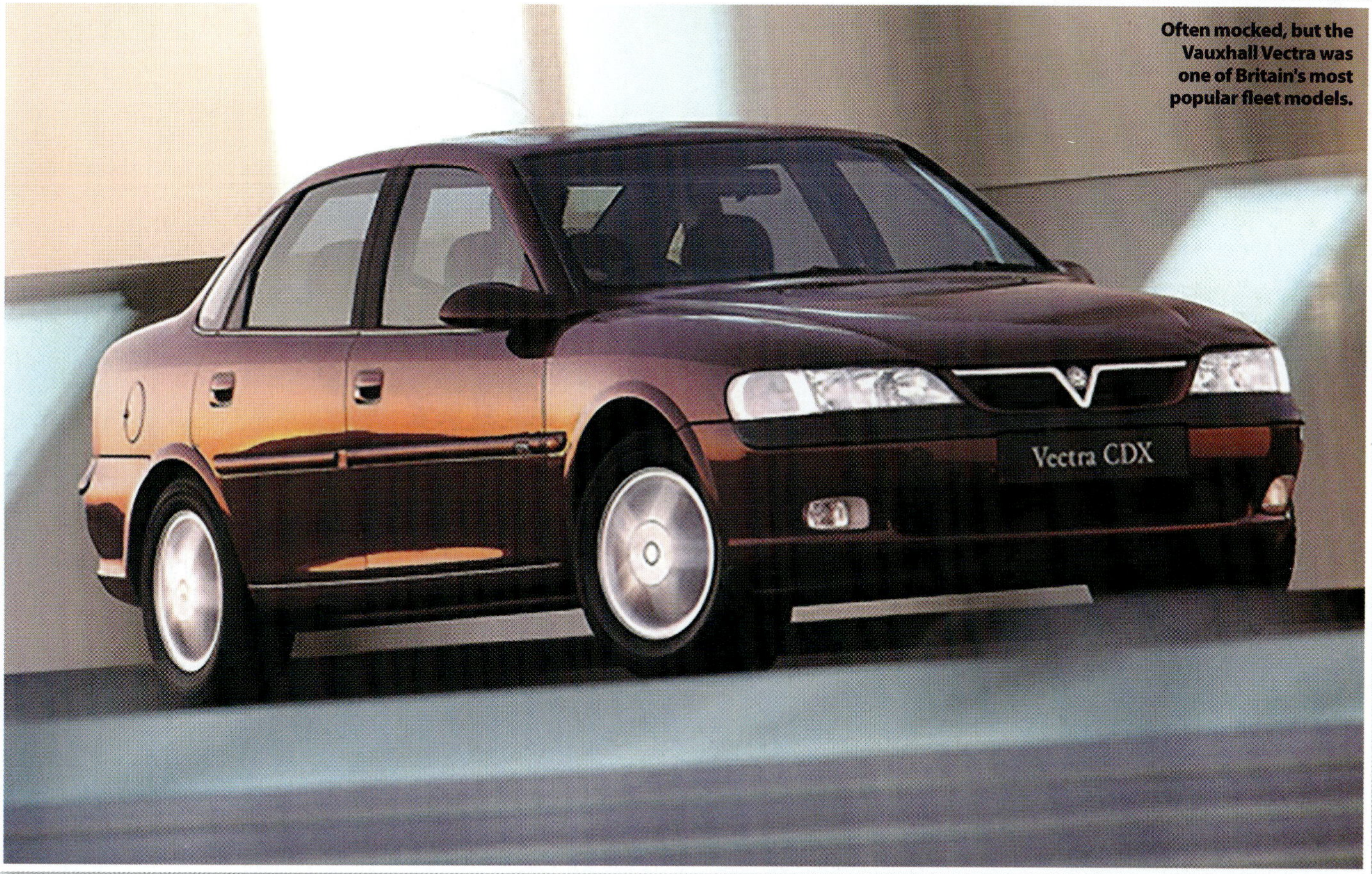

Often mocked, but the Vauxhall Vectra was one of Britain's most popular fleet models.

cash in on the idea that people would buy anything with a Ford badge, and the heavy revisions of 1996 to create the Escort Mk6 fell rather under the radar in the light of stiff competition from the Peugeot 306. Shame really, because those final Escorts were much better cars than you'd expect from their predecessors. But it was the Escort's successor that really changed the game. The Focus was the car that set the pace for the new Millennium.

The 1990s were also arguably the high water mark for our own car industry – with British Aerospace-owned Rover creating a number of premium models in part through its association with Honda and in part through its own ingenuity. The R8 series of 200 and 400 were sharply styled, upmarket cars that made us feel proud to buy British again. The 600 also genuinely took the fight from the Mondeo class to Germans such as the BMW 3-series, and while the 800 was perhaps a little past its best, its successor the 75 was a fitting final act to the last mainstream British motor manufacturer. With the finest walnut and leather atmosphere this side of Bentleys costing five or six times more, the Rover 75 hit the spot perfectly. It's just a shame that it was exactly the car a very small section of society wanted, with Rover losing fleet sales to reps who didn't want to arrive at client meetings in 1957.

Those sales reps instead found themselves, nine times out of ten, behind the wheel of the aforementioned Ford Mondeo or its deadliest rival; the Vauxhall Vectra. Introduced in 1995 to replace the Mondeo, it was famously savaged on BBC Top Gear by motoring pundit Jeremy Clarkson, who damned the Vectra with the faintest possible praise. Truth was that there was very little about the Vauxhall Vectra that was objectively bad, with the exception of its seats – but that it was so unforgivably average, and such a small step forward over the outgoing Mk3 Cavalier, that the accepted wisdom of the motoring press and public was that Vauxhall could have done better. Vauxhall itself agreed, with a revision for 1999 that incorporated 2500 individual improvements – none of which were visible to the naked eye or detectable by the driver.

Small wonder then that Vectra drivers had their eyes on something better – and the residual values of the German opposition meant that more and more companies were prepared to consider offering their travelling salesmen cars like

Small SUVs such as Land ROver's Freelander became the new in-thing.

The car that really showed that Ford meant business was the Focus. Intended to succeed the desperately dreary Mk5 and Mk6 Escorts, here was a car that looked good and drove better. The Escort might have been judged by two thousand and won, but the Focus was judged in 2000 to be a much better car.

the BMW 3-series or even – for those otherwise entitled to a top spec Mondeo or a Scorpio – the Mercedes-Benz E-class in entry level form. For those spending their own money, a similar sense of German solidity could be found in cars like the Volkswagen Passat – or further down the corporate ladder, the eternal trustworthiness of the Volkswagen Golf.

The attraction of the SUV as a family car had begun with the Range Rover based Land Rover Discovery, but intensified throughout the 1990s as manufacturers such as Vauxhall with its Frontera and Ford with its Maverick sought to attract a cut-price slice of the pie. The Land Rover Freelander of 1997 had the street cred to redefine the bottom end of the market, while premium manufacturers such as Mercedes and later BMW developed road-friendly SUVs of their own to take the fight to Range Rover and Discovery buyers.

As the 1990s shifted beyond the Millennium, the appeal of both German saloons and SUVs intensified, reshaping the automotive climate once more as buyers abandoned conventional mainstream saloon cars in their droves. ∎

Rover built upon its successes with the 75. It didn't get much more British, but Rover misjudged the tastes of its target customers.